Computer-Based Energy Management Systems

Technology and Applications

ENERGY SCIENCE AND ENGINEERING:
RESOURCES, TECHNOLOGY, MANAGEMENT
An International Series
EDITOR
JESSE DENTON
Belton, Texas

LARRY L. ANDERSON and DAVID A. TILLMAN (eds.), Fuels from Was
1977

A. J. ELLIS and W. A. J. MAHON, Chemistry and Geothermal Systen
1977

FRANCIS G. SHINSKEY, Energy Conservation through Control, 1978

N. BERKOWITZ, An Introduction to Coal Technology, 1979

JAN F. KREIDER, Medium and High Temperature Solar Processes, 1979

B. SØRENSEN, Renewable Energy, 1979

J. H. HARKER and J. R. BACKHURST, Fuel and Energy, 1981

STEPHEN J. FONASH, Solar Cell Device Physics, 1981

MALCOLM A. GRANT, IAN G. DONALDSON, and PAUL F. BIXLEY,
Geothermal Reservoir Engineering, 1982

W. F. KENNEY, Energy Conservation in the Process Industries, 1984

CHUN H. CHO, Computer-Based Energy Management Systems:
Technology and Applications, 1984

Computer-Based Energy Management Systems

Technology and Applications

CHUN H. CHO
Fisher Controls International, Inc.
Marshalltown, Iowa

1984

ACADEMIC PRESS, INC.

(Harcourt Brace Jovanovich, Publishers)
Orlando   San Diego   New York   London
Toronto   Montreal   Sydney   Tokyo

ACADEMIC PRESS, INC.
Orlando, Florida 32887

United Kingdom Edition published by
ACADEMIC PRESS, INC. (LONDON) LTD.
24/28 Oval Road, London NW1 7DX

Library of Congress Cataloging in Publication Data

Cho, Chun H.
  Computer-based energy management systems.

  (Energy science & engineering)
  Includes index.
  1. Industry--Energy conservation--Data processing.
I. Title. II. Series: Energy science and engineering.
TJ163.3.C46 1984   658.2'6   83-22341
ISBN 0-12-173380-7 (alk. paper)

PRINTED IN THE UNITED STATES OF AMERICA

84 85 86 87   9 8 7 6 5 4 3 2 1

To Max and Jean Billinger

For the encouragement and inspiration that allowed me to advance
my educational goals and career

Contents

3
Optimization Techniques

4
Selecting Computer Systems

5
Steam Plant Management

6
Electrical Power Management

7
Refrigeration Management Systems

8
Energy Accounting and System Diagnostics

9
Energy Management Opportunities in Selected Process Industries

10
Plant Study Procedures for Energy Conservation Projects

References   237

Index   239

Preface

The era of low-cost energy is undoubtedly a thing of the past. Today, energy management in industry is more than a fashionable subject, it is an outright necessity. The objective of an energy management system is simple enough to understand, but the means of improving plant energy efficiency is usually not so obvious.

Since the oil embargo of 1973, a major effort has been initiated by many energy-intensive process industries, as well as managers of large institutional buildings, to reduce energy consumption using the 1972 energy usage rates and costs as a base case.

It is generally true that from 1973 to 1975 most of the easily obtainable savings requiring low capital investments for energy conservation were achieved. These savings were mainly in the area of long-neglected housekeeping practices, for example, developing better insulation for steam pipes, starting steam trap maintenance programs, lowering thermostats, preventing steam leaks, and upgrading instrumentation for utility generation–distribution systems. Today, energy-intensive industries such as pulp and paper, petrochemical, and food processing are focusing their efforts on identifying, justifying, and implementing energy management systems to meet corporate mandates of 10–15% energy reduction per unit of production in addition to the 10–20% savings already realized since the embargo of 1973.

The trend is definitely toward a computer-based energy management system whose size will depend on the complexity of the utility complex. Computer technology has made major advances during the past 10–15 years. As a result, energy management and process control applications in many process industries are becoming more attractive because of the increasing reliability and decreasing cost of computer hardware. There have been significant activities both by users and manufacturers in the development and application of many pieces of software for controlling and optimizing utility complex and process unit operations.

The intent of this book is to present the material that is pertinent to planning, organizing, and developing computer-based energy management systems for industrial plants. The concepts, philosophical dissertations, and methodologies are developed and documented in such a way that readers can identify, select, and tailor their use of the book with respect to the specific needs of their plant.

Chapters 1–4 are devoted to giving the reader a good understanding of the concepts of computer-based energy management systems, approaches, and trends. In addition, the benefits of implementing advanced controls by upgrading plant instrumentation are highlighted in Chapter 2.

A comprehensive review of optimization techniques is included in Chapter 3, with particular emphasis on the techniques that can be readily adapted to solve complex energy allocation problems. These techniques have been available for many years, but until now we lacked the ability to apply them to engineering problems. In recent years, due to the availability of the process control computer, we have been able to handle optimization problems in an economical and timely manner so that real-time decisions can be made in the operation of a plant utility complex.

A thorough review of specifying and selecting a computer system is given in Chapter 4, from a user's as well as a supplier's point of view. Because of the tremendous proliferation of computer systems in the marketplace, it is no easy task to go about selecting a computer system that satisfies all of your functional requirements in both hardware and software. To a large extent, the success of a project depends on selecting the right computer and a supplier who can provide the necessary support.

Chapters 5–8 focus on the major utilities in process plants with respect to specific energy-savings potential and related computer functions. Steam, electric power, and refrigeration generally account for most of the plant energy budget. Computer systems have been playing a major role in reducing the consumption of such utilities.

Chapter 9 includes a summary of energy management opportunities in six selected industries: pulp and paper, steel, refining, chemical, textile, and energy production. The major differences in energy-savings potential among these industries are due to the process operations unique to each industry. The horizontal technology, as related to the basic utility systems discussed in Chapters 5–8, generally cuts across the boundaries of process operations.

A plant study to develop economic justification for a proposal is the single most important step toward competing for capital expenditures. Chapter 10 is intended to give the reader some ideas for analyzing plant data and developing a sound, documented basis for a potential energy savings.

This book covers a wide range of energy management topics and can be used to introduce practicing engineers to the field, to teach short courses in industrial energy systems, and as a reference book. In addition, the book should prove to be very beneficial as a supplementary reference book for undergraduate and graduate students in energy systems curricula. Because many of the optimization techniques mentioned in this book can be enhanced or need alternative solutions, it may spark further research ideas and developments in software applications.

List of Symbols

a, b, c	Constants	M	Total mass of combustion product
A	Surface area		
β	Beta ratio	M_c	Cooling-water flow
BD	Blowdown	M_e	Chilled-water flow
C	Constant, Cost	MDC	Master demand controller
C_d	Discharge coefficient	N	Number of stages
COP	Coefficient of performance	OE	Operating expense
C_t	Operating cost	P	Pressure
C_p	Specific heat of water	P_{fc}	Condenser-head pressure
CNF	Configuration function	PC	Pressure controller
D	Demand	PLC	Programmable logic controller
DSP	Desuperheating	Q	Condenser heat load, Gas flow
ε	Efficiency	Q_s	Mass flow rate of steam
F	Fuel flow rate	ROI	Return on investment
FT	Flow transmitter	S	Steaming rate, Scale factor
G_c	Generation cost	SC	Steam cost
I	Ideal	ΔT_c	Condenser temperature differential
H	Enthalphy		
ΔH	Change in enthalphy	ΔT_e	Temperature differential across evaporator
h_{fd}	Convective heat-transfer film coefficient		
HR	Actual heat rate	U	Heat-transfer coefficient
h_s	Scale heat-transfer coefficient	VPC	Valve position controller
K	Fuel cost	W_s	Compressor supplied energy
K_c	Compressor input energy	$\bar{x}$	n-dimensional vector
K_p	Pumping-cost factor for condenser	X	Fraction of excess air
		Y	Mole fraction
L	Load	Y_a	Adiabatic expression factor
LT	Level transmitter	Θ_m	Log-mean temperature difference
M	Maximum value	ρ	Density
		λ	Arbitrary multiplier

Computer-Based Energy Management Systems

Technology and Applications

1

Introduction

The most easily obtainable benefits requiring low capital investments for energy conservation have already been achieved by the energy-intensive industries since the oil embargo of 1973. In recent years computer-based energy management systems have played an increasingly important role in plantwide energy allocation and optimization to reduce production costs. Computer systems allow utility engineers to access real-time operating and performance information for energy-intensive equipment such as boilers, turbogenerators, compressors, and chillers and to optimize and control these systems to improve and maintain their energy utilization efficiencies. The application of computer systems also extends to many steam users, both in steam distribution systems and process areas.

A. Energy Management Activities and Approaches

Energy management activities include upgrading instrumentation to improve the efficiency of energy conversion efforts, optimizing load allocation, optimizing utility distribution, optimizing the allocation of fuels, managing electrical power and in-plant generation, and improving the energy efficiency of unit operations.

Successful energy management with computer systems requires careful planning and definition of each area included in the system with respect to the specific objective to be achieved. Every energy management project needs well-defined objectives and logical steps. The following guidelines may satisfy these needs.

(1) Identify and define the areas where energy management opportunities exist.
(2) Determine system functions and hardware and software requirements for each area.
(3) Make a cost–benefit analysis for the selected area of application. This phase is critical because a realistic savings projection is necessary to satisfy capital expenditure or return-on-investment (ROI) criteria. Such savings projections can be made by analyzing plant utility operating data or, in the absence of utility logs, by making a best engineering estimate.
(4) Prioritize the implementation plan based on the payback period of each application area.
(5) Make a plan to track the performance of and evaluate the energy management system in terms of cost savings upon system implementation.
(6) Select the system so that it can be expanded to integrate future energy systems.

B. Computer Functions

At the time the system specifications are developed it is important to focus on the following segments of the computer applications as applied to a given plant and its needs (Cho, 1975):

(1) data acquisition, calculation, and display;
(2) control philosophy and procedures [e.g., supervisory versus direct digital control (DDC), including backup requirements];
(3) identification of trends in plant data and performance variables;
(4) optimization techniques and procedures;
(5) logs and alarms; and
(6) management information systems.

There are many other concerns about the digital system that should be carefully evaluated in the course of the computer selection process (see Chapter 4).

C. System Implementation

Once the computer system specification is developed for energy management, there are several issues that should be addressed and clearly defined within the context of plant engineering expertise and available manpower. The major elements needing to be addressed at the time of project definition are design base and system specifications, system engineering, system integration, installation, and checkout, system startup and service, manufacturer-supplied software, custom software, spare parts, documentation, and costs.

D. Energy Conservation Opportunities

Most process industries, such as the petrochemical, pulp and paper, refining, and textile industries, use steam, electricity, cooling water, chilled water, compressed air, and many other forms and levels of utilities to process their products. Energy conservation opportunities generally exist in three areas in each utility energy system: generation, distribution, and consumption.

1. GENERATION

Steam, electricity, chilled water, and compressed air are generally either produced in the plant or purchased from outside utilities. Therefore, potential savings exist that may be obtained by minimizing the consumption of fuel or electricity in the generation of these utilities. It is not unusual to allocate as much as 60% of the cost of purchased fuel for steam generation and 20–30% for electrical power, either purchased or generated in-plant. In general, steam and/or electrical power must be consumed to generate chilled water, cooling tower water, compressed air, and many other utilities at the desired level of quality.

2. DISTRIBUTION

The distribution of generated energy is an extremely important factor in energy management systems. The objective of a distribution system is to deliver the required quantity and quality of energy to users without altering its original characteristics. Pressure, temperature, flow rate, and composition are a few of the essential elements that, depending on the type of utility, must be maintained to satisfy user specifications.

3. CONSUMPTION

The opportunity for saving energy is greater in the process that *uses* the utility. However, this is also the most difficult area for obtaining immediate results, because it requires an in-depth study to ensure that the conservation program would not interfere with the plant yield and product quality.

Many conservation opportunities exist in the area of by-product recovery. In many industries recovered and recycled heat energy constitute an important energy source and an opportunity for fuel conservation. The American Paper Institute reports that 20% of the energy needed to make pulp and paper is obtained from the burning and recycling of spent pulping liquid; an additional 8% of the required process steam is provided by the use of wood waste as fuel.

The basic objective of a conservation program is to seek out and implement energy-saving functions that reduce purchases of fuel and electricity while meeting plant demands.

E. Trends in Computer-Based Energy Management Systems

Computer technology has gone through a remarkable evolution since the earliest applications of computers in the process industries in the late 1950s. The mid-1960s saw the appearance of the first minicomputers, whose computational powers were comparable to those of the mainframe but whose cost had been greatly reduced.

In the early 1970s a second radical increase in computational power per dollar took place when the first microprocessors were introduced. Today microprocessor-based computers provide computational performance comparable to that of a small minicomputer at about one-third the cost. The introduction of microprocessors led to schemes for distributed control. It is now economically feasible to devote a microcomputer to an individual process instead of attempting to control an entire plant from a central computer. The distributed control scheme also allows a functional distribution of plant control and management objectives through use of a number of microprocessor-based intelligent controllers and devices communicating via an efficient highway system. This causes a significant increase in overall system reliability and total plant on-stream time. Hierarchical architectural schemes are a natural outgrowth of distributed system control.

1. CENTRALIZED COMPUTER SYSTEMS

In the early 1970s plant engineers began evaluating the feasibility of applying existing computer technology in plant energy conservation projects. A broad range of computerized process control capability existed, from simple programmable logic controllers (PLCs) to minicomputers for unit operations. Computer technology has a proven potential for reducing energy consumption and overall operating costs.

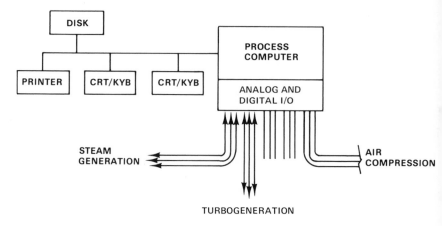

FIG. 1.1   A centralized computer system.

Most of the systems installed in the past were specified around centralized, or minicomputer, systems. These centralized computers have the necessary input and output interfaces and calculating ability to perform the functions required for effective energy management systems, including data acquisition, on-line equipment performance, advanced control implementation, and optimization routines. They also provide an efficient man–machine interface through video displays. Figure 1.1 depicts a centralized computer system.

The centralized computer approach is proving to be an effective way of interfacing with existing analog control systems to implement energy conservation projects. For example, a centralized computer system would be a desirable addition to a boiler house in which existing modern instrumentation provides combustion and turbine control and in which the optimization of steam and electrical power use is desired.

2. DISTRIBUTED CONTROL SYSTEMS
   (Manchon, 1982)

Many new installations in which a complete upgrading of the instrumentation system is required or in which there are a number of utility systems and process unit operations are geographically sepa-

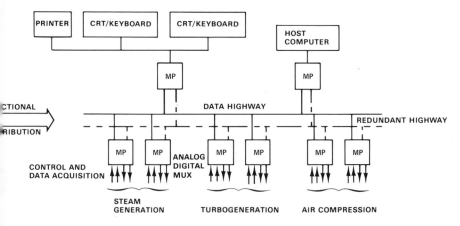

FIG. 1.2 A distributed computer system.

rated. In such cases, distributed control computer technology can now provide a cost effective implementation of energy management control and optimization functions. In distributed computer configurations such as the one shown in Fig. 1.2, the first level of control is performed by a microprocessor-based controller, whereas the monitoring, alarming, reporting, and supervisory calculations are done by a host computer at a central location.

The trend in the process industries is definitely toward hierarchical energy management systems in which a number of interrelated energy management functions can be implemented on an incremental basis, starting with process control applications and progressing through process optimization and management information systems. The distributed control system is well suited for integrating and managing many widely separated local utility areas. A typical geographic distribution of a number of elements in a utility complex is shown in Fig. 1.3.

3. LEVELS OF SYSTEM COMPLEXITY

The choice of hardware and system sophistication for a given energy management project is largely dictated by the complexity of tasks and by the necessity for trade-offs between economic benefits and capital investment.

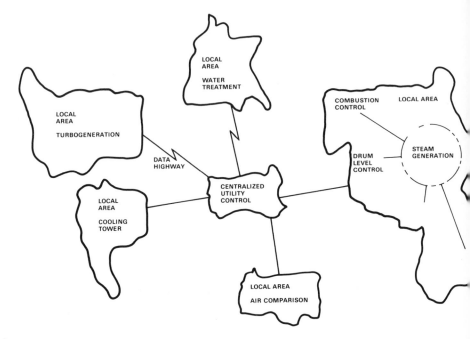

FIG. 1.3   Typical geographic distribution of a utility complex.

a. *Low-Level Complexity*

We shall use the powerhouse as an example of the concept of
system complexity. A plant having one to three small boilers (i.e.,
those with a maximum steaming rate under 30,000 lb/hr) and using
natural gas and oil may be defined as a system of low-level complexity. If the system analysis conducted by the plant engineer calls for
upgrading the boiler instrumentation, thus improving boiler efficiency, the task can be easily handled by either analog control devices or microprocessor-based controllers with operator stations for
the controller displays. There are many powerhouses in small industrial operations and institutions in which this first-level control enhancement is more than adequate to realize a good energy savings.

b. *Medium-Level Complexity*

If the boilers are firing multiple fuels, for example, gas, oil, or
waste products, and the automatic dispatch of fuels within the con-

straints of their availability is required, we need a system that is capable of obtaining the field data and generating supervisory commands to the first-level control devices. For automatic fuel dispatch control, which may require a console-based operator station with alarm and logging capability, either a minicomputer or distributed control is warranted.

c. High-Level Complexity

A large utility complex with multiple boilers and turbogenerators requires a system of high-level complexity. This may include the previously described systems in the low- and medium-level range of complexity, as well as optimization that, in the case of distributed control systems, requires a host computer. The optimization may involve automatic load allocations among the swing boilers, the automatic dispatch of multiple fuels, header pressure control, and turbogenerator management.

4. PLANTWIDE COMPUTER CONTROL
   (Williams, 1982)

In recent years a number of process industries (for example, steel and paper) have actively explored the concept of integrated plantwide control. These industries have played a leading role in the development of hierarchical distributed computer control and management systems. Each level in the system assumes a specific set of functions and responsibilities, focusing on the effective coordination of production planning and control, which provides the important link between business and process.

To date the most profitable result of plantwide control in the pulp and paper industry has been increased production. Other tangible benefits are reduced energy costs resulting from the integration of energy management functions in the system and reduced operating, maintenance, and capital costs.

The availability of low-cost, microprocessor-based digital systems for process monitoring and control can help to advance implementation plans for plantwide integrated computer control. Therefore, the basic control system for the steel industry (and similar industries) of the future involves a widely distributed set of separate but closely coordinated control functions carried out by an hierarchical system composed of many small and relatively inexpensive microcomputers at the plant interface. The first level of these plant interfaces, dedicated digital controllers, will be coordinated by a set of successively higher-level, and probably larger, computers communicating between the controllers through an efficient data communication highway.

The six levels proposed by the Purdue Laboratory for Applied Industrial Control as a specification for an integrated plantwide computer control system for integrated steel mills are shown in Fig. 1.4, and the details of the functions to be incorporated in each level are given in the following lists.

a. *Levels 1 and 2: Direct Digital and Dedicated Control*

(1) *Control enforcement.* Maintains direct control of the plant units under surveillance; detects and responds to any emergency condition arising in the plant units.

(2) *System coordination and reporting.* Collects information on unit production, raw material, and energy use and transmits the information to higher levels; services the operator's man–machine interface.

(3) *Reliability assurance.* Performs self-diagnostics; updates any standby systems.

b. *Level 3A: Supervisory Control*

(1) *Control enforcement.* Responds to any emergency condition arising in the plant units under surveillance; optimizes the operation of units under control within the limits of the established production schedule; carries out all established operational schemes or operating practices in connection with the processes involved.

(2) *System coordination and reporting.* Collects and·maintains data on production, inventory, raw material, and energy usage for the units under control; maintains communications with higher and lower levels; services the man–machine interfaces for the units involved.

(3) *Reliability assurance.* Performs diagnostics on itself and lower-level machines; updates all standby systems.

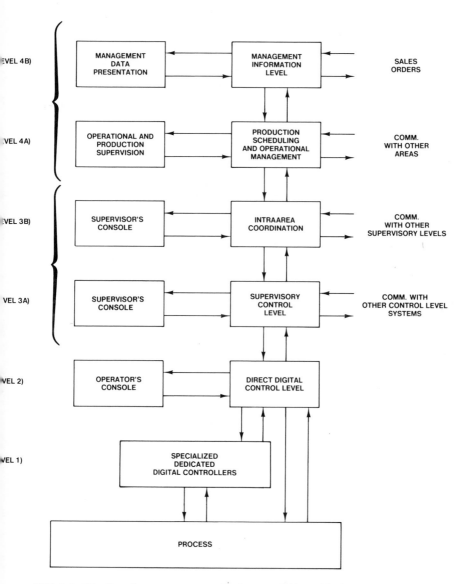

FIG. 1.4 Distributed computer system for the overall hierarchical computer control structure of an integrated steel mill. (From Williams, 1982.)

c. *Level 3B: Intra-area Coordination*

  (1) *Production scheduling.* Establishes the immediate production schedule for its own area, including transportation needs; locally optimizes the costs for its individual production area while carrying out the production schedule established by the production control computer system (Level 4A), that is, minimizes energy usage or maximizes production.

  (2) *System coordination and reporting.* Makes area production reports; uses and maintains area practice files; collects and maintains area data on production, inventory, raw materials usage, and energy usage; maintains communications with higher and lower levels of the heirarchy; collects operations data and performs off-line analysis as required by the engineering functions; services the man–machine interface for the area; carries out necessary personnel functions such as coordinating vacation and work schedules and keeping track of the union line of progression.

  (3) *Reliability assurance.* Performs diagnostics on itself and lower-level functions.

d. *Level 4A: Production Scheduling and Operational Management*

  (1) *Production scheduling.* Establishes the basic production schedule; modifies the production schedule for all units based on the order in which streams are received, energy constraints, and power demand levels; determines the optimum inventory level of goods in the process at each storage point (the criteria used are the trade-offs between customer service (i.e., a short delivery time) and the capital cost of the inventory itself, as well as the trade-offs between operating costs and the costs of carrying the inventory level. This is an off-line function.); modifies the production schedule whenever major interruptions in production occur in downstream units, where such interruption will affect preceding or succeeding units.

  (2) *Plant coordination and operational data reporting.* Collects and maintains an inventory of raw material usage and availability and provides data to the purchasing department for

raw material order entry; collects and maintains data on overall energy use and transfers the information to the accounting department; collects data on the overall goods in process and maintains production inventory files; collects and maintains the quality control file; maintains an interface with the management level and with area level systems.

(3) *Reliability assurance.* Runs self-check and self-diagnostic routines and diagnostics on lower-level machines.

e. *Level 4B: Intracompany Communications Control System*

(1) *System coordination and reporting.* Maintains interfaces with plant and company management, sales personnel, the accounting and purchasing departments, and the production scheduling level (4A); supplies production and status information (in the form of regular production and status reports and on-line inquiries) to plant and company management, sales personnel, and the accounting and purchasing departments; supplies order status information to sales personnel.

(2) *Reliability assurance.* Performs self-diagnostic checks.

f. *Requirements for Man–Machine Interfaces for Industrial Control Systems*

(1) There could be a single man–machine interface station capable of providing all the necessary functions at any one location. It should be located within easy reach of a seated operator. Redundant displays are required for reliability, not for additional presentations.

(2) Information about overall process operation should be conveyed to the operators as exceptions occur.

(3) Compact methods of indicating the overall state of a process should take advantage of pattern recognition display techniques. These should be machine-implemented if possible.

(4) Data should be available in grouped displays that convey the functioning of small subsystems of the process unit.

(5) Alarm systems should be simplified into hierarchies that can be selectively suppressed as a function of the operating state.

(6) The display of trends or past histories of variables is essential for operator guidance; hard copy is not required by the operators but is required for record purposes.

(7) Analog displays convey qualitative information the most rapidly. However, digital displays should be used when quantitative detail is important, and the two forms should be intermixed as required.

(8) In computer control systems more use should be made of derived variables to measure process performance. Operators must increasingly work with derived variables such as efficiency, cost, profit, yield rather than with simple flows, pressures, and temperatures.

F. Energy Management Organization

Energy management programs, to be successful, require the participation of management from top to bottom, from the corporate chairman to the line supervisor and plant operating personnel. Energy management organizations responsible for all aspects of energy conservation programs should be structured at the corporate and plant levels with clear-cut objectives in mind and a precise idea of the results to be obtained.

1. CORPORATE ENERGY COMMITTEES
(Bauman, 1975)

In multiplant companies a corporate energy committee should be organized to include an energy conservation coordinator, to act as the catalyst of the corporate conservation effort, as well as engineering, purchasing, and public relations personnel. In addition, it may be necessary to secure an outside utility systems consultant as a committee member or to use corporate engineering personnel who have expertise in utility systems.

The corporate energy committee usually serves in an advisory capacity, coordinating, monitoring, and assisting energy conservation programs and projects at the plant level. The functions of the corporate energy committee may include the following.

(1) Develops, proposes, and initiates methods and programs to ensure the optimum utilization of all energy sources.

(2) Helps ensure a continuous energy supply by seeking available and alternative sources for plant needs.

(3) Evaluates and recommends standby energy systems for critical services.

(4) Keeps abreast of legislative activities at both the state and federal levels that affect fuels, energy, environmental regulations, and investment tax credits for energy-related projects.

(5) Prepares position statements for corporate management regarding legislation and other government actions that influence fuel and energy matters.

(6) Serves as a central clearinghouse for coordinating the activities of individual plant energy committees.

(7) Monitors energy audit reports from the individual plants so that corporate policy or mandates on energy conservation efforts can be measured.

(8) Organizes and sponsors periodic energy conservation conferences and workshops for the purpose of disseminating energy conservation accomplishments and case histories to individual plants.

(9) Publishes periodic reports on committee activities and circulates them to corporate, division, and plant management.

(10) Participates in outside technical organizations that promote the exchange of energy conservation programs and technical information.

(11) Sponsors energy management seminars, inviting outside speakers, for the benefit of corporate and plant energy conservation committee members and engineering personnel. The subjects for seminars may include selecting energy-efficient plant equipment, designing energy-efficient processes, and improving energy efficiency by upgrading instruments, applying advanced control, and computer applications.

2. PLANT ENERGY COMMITTEES

In many respects the responsibilities of the plant energy committee are similar to those of the corporate committee. However, the obvious difference is that the plant energy committee is responsible for *implementing* the energy conservation programs, including the capital projects for energy savings. Therefore, the plant energy committee is in many instances directly accountable for the results and the corporate return-on-investment (ROI) objective.

An effective plant energy committee has a few people and is chaired by the plant manager, the plant engineer, or someone in a comparable position of responsibility. This is an action group that must make timely decisions to develop specific energy conservation programs, define tasks and functions, assign the proper manpower, and measure the results. For energy projects involving sizable capital, the committee should prioritize the projects according to ROI, risks, and long-term effects.

No single plant energy committee structure will satisfy the needs of all individual plants. For a multiplant company with a division that is responsible for a number of plants producing allied products, the plant energy committee may include a division energy coordinator, a utility and maintenance superintendent, a purchasing agent, a process (operations) engineer, and an environmental engineer.

The following are some of the recommended functions and responsibilities for a plant energy committee.

(1) Customizes programs recommended by the corporate energy committee for the individual plant.
(2) Develops available and economical sources of energy for plant use.
(3) Reports periodically on the progress of energy conservation programs and circulates the reports to other plants within the company.
(4) Coordinates activities with the plant environmental department so that the energy conservation programs will not violate the standards set by state and federal agencies.
(5) Analyzes the manpower requirements of the plant to derive the maximum benefit from capital projects involving new equipment, for example, computer-based energy management systems.

2

Energy Conservation Opportunities through Better Control

There are two ways in which computerized process control can improve energy efficiency in any process: the regulation and control of process variables closer to a desired value and the application of optimization techniques to allocate plantwide energy loads, resulting in a minimum total energy cost. Presented in this chapter are a number of topics that focus on the philosophy of control, the application of advanced control strategies and procedures, and the potential application of optimization techniques.

A. Philosophy of Control for Energy Processes

In processes that contribute to performance degradation, thus incurring higher operating costs, there are two major reasons for en-

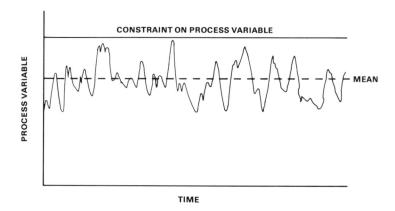

FIG. 2.1   Process variable response prior to application of advanced control.

ergy efficiency. First, many process control loops cannot maintain controlled variables at the desired set points because of inadequate instrumentation and control, e.g., many of these loops are on manual control. Second, as a consequence of the former problem, the process set points are not at optimum values.

Figure 2.1 shows one of the problems typically associated with inadequate instrumentation and control. Because of the instability in the control loop, the controlled variable has a large standard of deviation. Therefore, to avoid potential violations, the mean of the controller variable is set significantly below the constraint. It is desirable to operate the control loop as close as possible to the constraint because this will minimize the energy consumption of the process.

To improve the unstable loop, one must first review and analyze the existing instrumentation and control strategy; the process and instrumentation diagram is a good place to find this information. When the process characteristics and process disturbances are understood, a better control strategy can be implemented by improvement of the control loop or by the selection and application of the following advanced control techniques: feedforward, cascade, calculation, decoupling, adaptive gain, and material and energy balance.

The application of such control techniques usually leads to improved controlled variable response. Figure 2.2, when compared

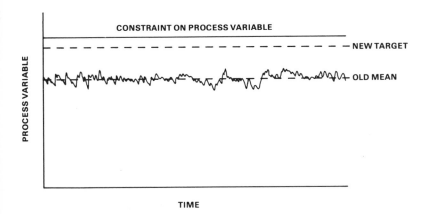

FIG. 2.2   Response after improved control was applied to Fig. 2.1.

with Fig. 2.1, illustrates improved closed-loop response characteristics.

Further improvement may be achieved by applying a priori optimization, which simply means moving controlled variable targets
closer to the constraints. This optimization technique reduces energy consumption. Figure 2.3 shows the final step that moves the
controlled variable to the system constraint.

The following are good examples for the application of stabilizing
control and a priori optimization to reduce energy costs.

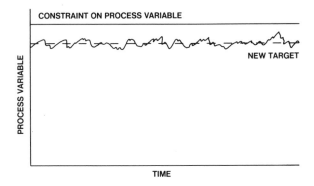

FIG. 2.3   A priori optimization—improved process economics.

1. BOILER O_2 CONTROL

The constraint is the O_2 limit, which leads to incomplete combustion and to a greater increase in energy losses than that associated with stack O_2 losses.

2. BOILER BLOWDOWN CONTROL

The constraint is the maximum allowable level of total dissolved solids (TDS) in the boiler water. A properly designed automatic blowdown control system can maintain the blowdown close to this maximum allowable level, thus minimizing blowdown. Blowdown reduction conserves heat in the boiler water, conserves the chemical used to treat boiler makeup water, and reduces labor costs.

3. TIE-LINE CONTROL

The maximum constraint is the demand limit on purchased electricity. Violating this constraint results in an increased demand rate, usually for the next 12 months. By operating near the purchased kilowatt target, the system minimizes the costly condensing generation in the plant.

4. HEATER OUTLET TEMPERATURE CONTROL

The minimum constraint is the temperature which satisfies process energy demands. Operating near the constraint allows for improvement in heater efficiency by reducing internal heater temperatures.

Combustion control systems provide good examples of the upgrading of instrumentation and the introduction of advanced control strategy. Many industrial boilers installed before the oil embargo of 1973 are instrumented with minimum control hardware. Because of low fuel costs, the justification for sophisticated control strategies and instrumentation did not exist at that time. However, in view of today's escalating fuel cost, upgrading boiler instrumentation, e.g., boiler sizes with capacities over 40,000 lb/hr, yields a good return on investment.

B. Design Procedure for an Advanced Control System

To satisfy the control objective, the following procedure, which uses advanced control techniques, is offered as a general guideline for the design of a new control system or the improvement of an existing one.

Step 1. Define the controlled variable from the point of view of controllability, including the requirements for process measurement and process economics.

Step 2. Choose the manipulated variables which have the greatest impact on the process to be controlled. The sensitivity analysis of the controlled variable to the manipulated variables can be evaluated using process models and simulation techniques.

Step 3. Define the process disturbances which are responsible for process upsets. The sensitivity analysis of process upsets caused by the disturbances should be investigated by simulation techniques or on-line process testing. It is also important to recognize which disturbances are measurable with analyzers or sensors, so that the flexibility of an advanced control can be evaluated.

Step 4. Using the preceding steps, pair the controlled variables with the manipulated ones.

Step 5. Develop the control algorithms for feedforward and/or decoupling control. These algorithms are usually based on the steady-state material and/or energy balances.

Step 6. Define the dynamic compensation needs associated with feedforward control strategy. This definition is usually based on well-established guidelines, experience, process testing, or possible system simulation.

Step 7. Design the operator interface.

Step 8. Select the equipment necessary to implement the control schemes.

Step 9. Implement the control system. In an analog system, scaling is a part of the implementation, whereas in a digital system, data base design and generation are a part of the implementation.

Step 10.   Train the operators.
Step 11.   Start up and tune the system.
Step 12.   Prepare documentation.

C. Applying Optimization Techniques

Once the control system is properly designed and implemented, the first level of process optimization is completed (Cho, 1981). The second level of the optimization problem focuses on determining optimum targets for a number of the controlled variables, e.g., distributing the plant steam load between the parallel boilers so that the incremental steam cost is minimized. In this hierarchical management system the local controllers (in this case the boiler masters) respond to the optimizer-generated remote set-point signals to bias each boiler with respect to the level of steam generation.

Traditionally, the problem of global optimization has not been considered because the operator was unable to determine optimum targets. Therefore, the set points are not at optimum values. The problem is typically a multivariable one which requires a system to handle extensive calculations and optimum solutions.

The automated solution of the problem involves the application of an optimization procedure. An objective function is formulated to solve for either a maximum or minimum value by an optimization routine subject to the system's operating constraints. This method for achieving improvements is classified as a *constrained set-point optimization.*

1. BOILER LOAD ALLOCATION

This method minimizes the cost of steam production in a steam plant complex where there are a number of swing boilers with reserve capacities.

2. BOILER FUEL OPTIMIZATION

The purpose of fuel optimization is to minimize the cost of meeting the steam demand on multiple fuel boilers.

3. TURBOGENERATOR LOAD ALLOCATION, OR TIE-LINE OPTIMIZATION

In an industrial plant in which the total electrical power demand is satisfied by the cogeneration complex, the electrical load can be allocated among the turbogenerators, based on the heat rates of condensing generations. If a tie-line set point is included in the decision-making process, i.e., on make or buy decisions, then the overall goal is to minimize the cost of total electrical energy.

4. TURBOGENERATOR EXTRACTION FLOW ALLOCATION

The purpose of this optimization is to maximize the production of electricity by extraction flows in the multiple extraction turbo-generators. This maximization is achieved by producing steam for a particular header from those turbines that are most efficient in the production of electricity, i.e., those which generate the most electricity per pound of extracted steam.

In Chapter 3 a number of optimization techniques will be described. Particular emphasis will be placed on total cost allocation techniques and on individual unit cost allocation technique for constrained set-point optimization solutions.

D. Example of an Advanced Control System

The concept of advanced control, as discussed in Section A, has become an important system design consideration in every facet of process control applications. Because of the advances in microprocessor technology and a marked decrease in hardware cost, the implementation of advanced control with a flexible digital controller is very economically attractive (Cho, 1982).

1. BOILER-DRUM-LEVEL CONTROL

Boiler-drum-level control will serve as an introduction to the concept of advanced control. We shall begin with a simple feedback control (single-element feedwater control), and advance to a three-element feedwater control, an advanced control technique incorporating feedforward, feedback, and cascade to control drum level.

In the powerhouse operations, the boiler-drum-level control system is a vital subsystem in the production of steam. In response to steam demand fluctuations, the feedwater-control system must operate properly by maintaining its mid-drum set point. The high drum level causes the steam quality to exceed its allowable moisture content, whereas the low drum level can cause the boiler tubes to burn out.

We shall next discuss the concepts related to feedback, feedforward, and cascade with respect to each system's performance characteristics.

a. *Drum-Level Control with Feedback Only*
   (Single-Element Feedwater Control)

In traditional feedback control, a controller takes action only when a measured variable deviates from its set point. Figure 2.4 shows a simple feedback control loop for a boiler drum; when the level drops below its set point, the controller will trim the feedwater valve to compensate.

Single-element feedwater control for boiler-drum level is problematic if one controls the set point in response to rapid steam-demand changes. Since boiler-drum level is a major variable to be controlled (i.e., it must stay within ±2 in. of the set point), most of the boilers which are instrumented, retrofitted, or upgraded generally include feedforward and cascade-control strategies and associated instrumentation.

b. *Drum-Level Control with Feedforward and Feedback*
   (Two-Element Feedwater Control)

If one can predict what will happen when a load change occurs, either upstream or downstream from the control loop, then it is possible to take corrective action before an upset occurs. In Fig. 2.5, for example, removing steam from the boiler drum directly affects its level; it is possible, therefore, to measure steam flow, calculate its effect on the level, and adjust the feedwater flow before the level changes.

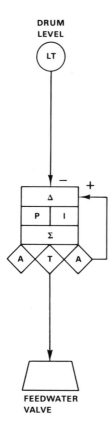

FIG. 2.4   Single-element feedwater control. LT, level transmitter; P, proportional control mode; I, integral control mode; A, local set point; T, transfer. (From Cho, 1982.)

Feedforward control is an inherently open loop, because the controlled variable (level, in this case) is not measured for control purposes. Since feedforward control cannot compensate for mathematical inaccuracies in the process model, instrument measurement errors, or unmeasured process disturbances, this control method is rarely used by itself. In this example, manual action would frequently be required to prevent a dry drum at the low extreme or an overflow at the high extreme. Instead, feedforward signals are generally used in combination with a feedback-control system, as shown in Fig. 2.6.

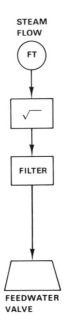

FIG. 2.5   Feedwater-drum-level control. FT, flow transmitter. (From Cho, 1982.)

In the example of boiler-drum-level control, additive feedforward compensation can solve several problems in the feedback loop. Under feedback control alone, increasing the steam load eventually causes the drum level to drop. Therefore, the controller should open the feedwater valve to compensate. One problem associated with this method is the time lag through the boiler, which retards response. Another difficulty arises from sudden increases in steam demand which temporarily lower drum pressure and increase the volume of steam bubbles. This causes a "swell" in the drum which raises the apparent level.

Feedforward control can be applied by measuring the steam flow rate, applying a scale factor to relate flow to the change in drum level, and adding the resulting signal to the feedback level-control signal. An increase in steam load, therefore, will cause the valve to open before the drum level changes. Lead–lag compensation can be used dynamically to match the feedforward signal to the process response.

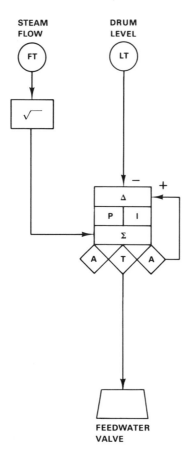

FIG. 2.6   Two-element feedwater control. (From Cho, 1982.)

Because additive feedforward control is relatively simple, it is possible to incorporate all the necessary hardware elements into a single controller. Such controllers, available from several manufacturers, accept two or more process signals, include summer circuitry, and provide smooth transfers between manual and automatic modes.

In practice, additive feedforward control can be tuned with relatively few adjustments. The scale is the prime setting, since it determines the relative influence of the feedforward signal on the control action. In some systems a constant is known in advance; in others, it is not directly predictable and must be tuned. Its precise setting is not critical, however, because the feedback loop still references its output signal to the set point. A switch allows one to select forward or reverse action (addition or subtraction of the feedforward signal), and a breakpoint threshold value establishes a threshold on feedforward action. Below the threshold, feedforward signals have no effect on the controller's output.

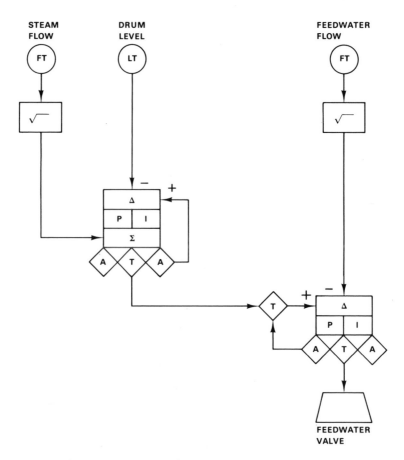

FIG. 2.7   Three-element feedwater control. (From Cho, 1982.)

c. *Drum-Level Control with Feedforward, Feedback, and Cascade (Three-Element Feedwater Control)*

As boilers become larger in capacity, economic considerations make it desirable to minimize drum size and increase velocities in the water and steam systems. A three-element feedwater-control system should be installed on larger boilers, as well as on smaller boilers that are subject to very wide and rapid load changes. The three-element system, shown in Fig. 2.7, maintains water input equal to steam output and uses drum level, steam flow, and feedwater flow as process variables to control the steam-drum water level.

The steam-flow signal, which indicates the basic demand for feedwater flow, is summed with the output of the drum-level controller, and the summer output is the total feedwater-demand signal to the feedwater-flow controller. The flow controller compares the process variable signal of feedwater flow with the total feedwater-demand signal, and provides corrective action to position the feedwater-control valve. The three-element feedwater-control system restores drum water level at virtually all boiler loads, even with varying feedwater-header pressure.

The introduction of a feedwater controller makes it possible to introduce a cascade-control system in which the level controller output signal becomes a remote set-point signal to the flow controller. Therefore, the feedwater delivery is a function of the remote set-point signal only; it is completely independent of any inlet feedwater-header pressure variations upstream of the feedwater valve.

E. Examples of Energy Conservation Control

There are many opportunities, both in the plant utility complex and in production areas, for conserving energies through an automatic control. Header-pressure control and automatic boiler blowdown control will be presented as examples of specific application concepts and economic benefits.

1. HEADER-PRESSURE CONTROL

Steam distribution headers and their pressure set points are assigned to satisfy the steam users by providing the quantities of steam needed at specific pressures and temperatures (Shinskey, 1978).

Production rate has a direct influence over the changes in header pressure. When production is running at full capacity, the assigned pressure may not be high enough to satisfy all the users. In this case, insufficient pressure is indicated by wide-open control valves. However, when the production is low, valves are throttled and could perhaps accept a much lower pressure.

Recognizing that throttling is an irreversible process, it would seem desirable to force control valves further open, while maintaining control of their individual variables. This can be done by reducing header pressure, as production rates cause valves to close. To satisfy all users, however, the pressure must be held at a point that will keep the most wide-open valve just short of fully open.

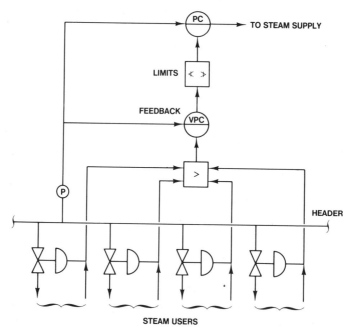

FIG. 2.8   Header pressure control, where VPC is the valve position controller and PC is the pressure controller. (From Shinskey, 1978.)

The system shown in Fig. 2.8 accomplishes this. The positions of all the control valves supplied by the header are compared in a high selector. The position of the most open valve is then maintained at the 90 to 95% open position by a controller which adjusts the set point of the header-pressure controller between specified limits. Rapid fluctuations in pressure are not allowed, as they will upset all the users. Therefore, the valve-position controller must do its job slowly. It must have little or no proportional action and an integral time of several minutes. Because of its slow response, the valve-position controller cannot hold the selected valve position tightly at the set point but only keep its average position there. Short-term upsets will be quickly countered by the action of the pressure controller, while long-term variations in load will cause header pressure to rise or fall slowly. Using the measured pressure as feedback to the valve-position controller will properly condition it whenever limits are encountered or when pressure is controlled at a locally set value.

2. BLOWDOWN CONTROL

Continuous or intermittent boiler blowdown is used to control the level of total dissolved solids in boiler water. Therefore, blowdown is an integral part of the control necessary to ensure proper operation of the boiler. The level of these dissolved solids is directly related to the scale-forming tendency of the water, and carry-over of solids in the steam lines can impair system operation and damage the steam-driven equipment.

A number of interrelated factors determine the required blowdown rate. These include the characteristics of the makeup water (e.g., total hardness, silica, and total solids), the amount of condensate return, and the steaming rate. Any variation in any one of these three factors effects the amount of blowdown required and makes manual control more difficult.

Figure 2.9 depicts a typical distribution of the frequency of blowdown occurrence, under manual and automatic control, as conductance is varied. The average value for the manual blowdown control is about 80% of the maximum allowable value, which is maintained by excess blowdown. The automatic blowdown system can control the blowdown close to the maximum allowable constraint line so that the blowdown is minimized. This is a good example of a priori optimization, as discussed in Section 2.A. On average, the blow-

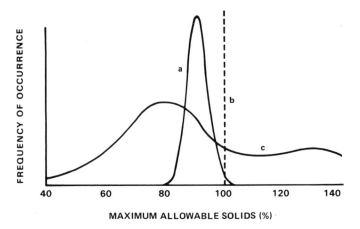

FIG. 2.9   Manual (curve c) versus automatic (curve a) blowdown control. Line b denotes maximum allowable solids level.

down with an automatic control saves from 12 to 18% of the boiler water chemicals alone.

An automatic blowdown-control system continuously monitors the boiler water with an analyzer (i.e., a conductivity analyzer) and adjusts the rate of blowdown with a controller. A typical automatic blowdown-control system is shown in Fig. 2.10. It consists of a measurement device (analyzer plus transmitter), a controller [either on/off or standard proportional plus integral (PI) flow controller], and a control valve. In many instances, the flash tank associated with the blowdown can recover as much as 20% of the blowdown as low-pressure steam.

One may begin to calculate the savings which result from the installation of an automatic blowdown-control system by determining the normal N and maximum M cycles of concentration as

$$N = \frac{\text{conductivity of boiler water}}{\text{conductivity of makeup water}}$$

and

$$M = \frac{\text{maximum conductivity limit}}{\text{conductivity of makeup water}}.$$

Next, the blowdown (BD) rate may be calculated using an industry-accepted formula:

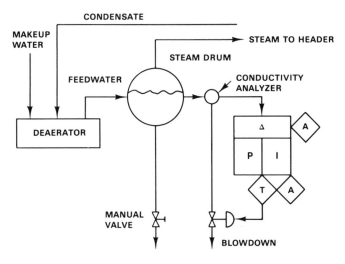

FIG. 2.10   Automatic blowdown control.

$$BD_{normal} = \text{average steam rate}/(N - 1) \quad \text{lb/hr},$$

$$BD_{max} = \text{average steam rate}/(M - 1) \quad \text{lb/hr}.$$

Then excess blowdown can be computed using the equation

$$\Delta BD = BD_{normal} - BD_{max} \quad \text{lb/hr},$$

with the cost of blowdown determined by the cost of water ($/hr) and the cost of heat:

$$\Delta \text{Btu saving} = (h_{bw} - h_{mw})/\text{boiler efficiency} \quad \text{Btu/lb},$$

where h_{bw} and h_{mw} are enthalpies of blowdown water and makeup water, respectively. The following are hypothetical data, which may be used to calculate possible savings.

Average boiler steaming rate	125,000 lb/hr
Boiler efficiency	80%
Fuel cost no. 6 oil	$4.00/$10^6$ Btu
Operating hours	8400 hr/yr
Makeup water	$0.50/1000 gal
Enthalpy of blowdown water (h_{bw})	450 Btu/lb
Enthalpy of makeup water (h_{mw})	28 Btu/lb
N	24
M	37

We now insert these figures into our equations, with the following results:

$$\text{energy savings} = \left(\frac{125{,}000}{23} - \frac{125{,}000}{36}\right)\left(\frac{450 - 28}{0.80}\right)$$

$$\times \ (\$4/\bar{M} \ \text{Btu})(8400) = \$34{,}784/\text{yr},$$

$$\text{water savings} = \left(\frac{125{,}000}{23} - \frac{125{,}000}{36}\right)\left(\frac{1}{8.34}\right)$$

$$\times \ (\$0.50/1000 \ \text{gal})(8400) = \$988/\text{yr},$$

$$\text{total} = \$34{,}785.00 + \$988.00 = \$35{,}773/\text{yr}.$$

3

Optimization Techniques

Many optimization techniques have been developed by different investigators for both linear and nonlinear problems. A number of these optimization methods have been successfully applied in the solution of objective functions that define energy systems.

After formulating the equations that define the performance and costs of a system and specifying the controlled and independent variables, the system engineer must select the optimization technique best suited for the problem at hand. Recent advances in and increased availability of digital systems have led to their widespread and effective use in process control applications. The implementation of control algorithm and optimization procedures have also been accepted with good results.

The goal of optimization is to find a solution that satisfies a system's preassigned performance criteria without violating any of that system's constraints. Allowing for certain adjustable parameters, the optimization procedure must generate a solution that meets the system objective.

The performance requirement often takes the form of a performance index that must be maximized or minimized. An example of this is a least-cost operation in a steam plant that results in a minimum fuel cost while satisfying the plant's steam demand. The performance index can be expressed as follows: given the function $f(\bar{x})$, where $\bar{x}$ is an n-dimensional vector of the form $(x_1, x_2, x_3, \ldots, x_n)$, find the vector $\bar{x}_m$ that minimizes or maximizes $f(\bar{x})$ subject to k constraint relationships $g_k(\bar{x}) \geq C_k$, where C_k are constants.

To formulate the optimization problem, the performance index $f(\bar{x})$ should be defined in terms of independent system variables. The objective function $f(\bar{x})$ represents a hypersurface in an $(n + 1)$-dimensional space. The system constraints are limits on individual variables and, in a complex system, incorporate several variables. The constraint relationships represent hypersurfaces that confine the solution space.

A. A Survey of Optimization Techniques

There are many different techniques for determining the external value of a function (Deliyannides, 1968). Some of those most frequently used are briefly discussed here.

1. DIRECT CALCULATION METHOD

When there are a small number of variables, each with a finite number of values, it is possible with a limited domain to calculate the performance index directly for various sets of the variables and to retain that set resulting in the highest value of the objective function. The calculation is repeated until the objective function cannot be improved any more. However, this method becomes prohibitive as the number of variables increases.

2. CLASSICAL DIFFERENTIAL CALCULUS METHOD

Another well-known method, classical differential calculus can be found in any basic textbook. If $f(\bar{x})$ has continuous partial derivatives, then the extremum of the function can be found by setting all the partial derivatives of f with respect to x_1 equal to zero and solving the equations simultaneously as

$$\partial f/\partial x_i|_{x_r \text{ for } r \neq i} = 0, \qquad i = 1, 2, ..., n. \tag{3.1}$$

The values of x_i obtained by solving the above n simultaneous equations give the extremum points of the function. Whether these points are maximum or minimum can be determined from the sign of higher-order derivatives. Unfortunately, if the function is multinodal, there is no way to determine whether the extremum point is relative or absolute. This must be done by testing the value of the function at each extremum point. Although this method cannot handle inequality constraints directly, through a modification of this method equality constraints can be handled as discussed next.

3. LAGRANGE MULTIPLIER METHOD

When the function $f(\bar{x}) = 0$ must be solved subject to the constraints $g_j(\bar{x}) = 0$, where $j = 1, 2, ..., m$, $m < n$, then the Lagrange multiplier method introduces m arbitrary multipliers $\lambda_1, \lambda_2, ..., \lambda_m$ and forms the Lagrange function

$$F(\bar{x}, \lambda) = f(\bar{x}) + \sum_{i=1}^{m} \lambda_1 g_i(\bar{x}).$$

It turns out that the necessary conditions for an unconstrained extremum of $F(\bar{x}, \lambda)$, namely, the vanishing of F's partial derivatives, are also the necessary conditions for a constrained extremum of $f(\bar{x})$. By using the n equations $\partial F/\partial x_1 = 0$ and the m equations $g_j(\bar{x}) = 0$, we can solve for n unknowns of x and m unknowns of λ. Actually, only those values of x that are the coordinates of the extremum point are of interest.

4. LINEAR AND NONLINEAR PROGRAMMING

When the objective function is in the linear form

$$f(\bar{x}) = \sum_{i=1}^{n} c_i x_i$$

and the constraints are in the form

$$\sum_{j=1}^{m} a_{ij} x_i \geq b_j$$

(with the additional constraint $x_1 \geq 0$), then the extrema of the function occur at the boundaries and the classical differential calculus method again fails. This is known as the *linear programming problem* and can be solved by the simplex method defined by Dantzig, which introduces m new variables $x_{n+1}, \ldots, x_{n+m}$. These *slack variables* are subject to the nonnegative constraint and are added to the inequality constraints to transform them into equality relationships. Any set of values $(x_1, x_2, x_3, \ldots, x_{n+m})$ that satisfies these quality relations is called a *feasible solution* of the linear programming problem. Of course, there are many feasible solutions and the one that optimizes the objective function is the optimal solution. The simplex method solves the problem in two conceptual stages. First, it gives a procedure that, starting with an arbitrary set of values, finds a feasible solution by iteration. Second, it gives a procedure for starting with a feasible solution and finding, by iteration, an optimal solution.

The geometric interpretation of the linear programming method holds that constraint relations define a set of hyperplanes that outline a solution in the n-dimensional space. The objective function is also a hyperplane, which is allowed to move within this solution space. The optimal point always lies at the intersection of two hyperplanes. The simplex solution method, starting at any point, finds itself at such an intersection and then proceeds from one intersection point to another until the optimum value of the objective function is found.

The limitation of this method is the linear form that the objective function and the constraints must take. In optimizing physical systems, this is a severe limitation. Extensions of this method to nonlinear objective functions have been tried with limited success. To date there is no general method of handling nonlinear constraint relationships.

5. DYNAMIC PROGRAMMING

Dynamic programming, which is a general procedure and philosophy rather than a mathematical algorithm, was developed by Bellman. It is used in optimization of discrete stage processes and is based on the principle of optimality. According to this principle, an optimal policy has the property that, whatever the initial state and initial decisions are in an N-stage process, the remaining decisions must constitute an optimal policy with regard to the state resulting from the first decision. The principle of optimality is formulated as follows: At the nth stage of an N-stage process a decision must be made to allocate a portion y_n of the total available resources x_n to obtain a return $g(y_n)$. The return on the remainder $(x_n - y_n)$ is $h(x_n - y_n)$. The quantity available for the next stage is assumed to be

$$x_{n+1} = ay_n + b(x_n - y_n). \tag{3.2}$$

At the end of n stages there are $N - n$ remaining stages, or decisions. The problem is finding an optimum function $f_{N-n}(x_n)$ that will give the maximum yield for the remaining $N - n$ stages, which have the starting value of x_n at the end of the nth stage, i.e.,

$$f_{N-n}(x_n) = \max[g(y_n) + h(x_n - y_n) + f_{N-(n+1)}(x_{n+1})]. \tag{3.3}$$

The solution is obtained through an iterative algorithm, starting at the last stage and proceeding backward toward earlier stages, retaining only the path that, regardless of the decisions made at earlier stages, will maximize the function $f_{N-n}(x_n)$ between stage n and the last stage N.

This method is very effective in processing discrete stages. The problem with applying this method in continuous processes lies in selecting the proper stages. Another disadvantage is that it cannot conveniently handle inequality constraints.

B. Review of Experimental Search Methods

Experimental search methods are characterized by a pragmatic approach that is willing to sacrifice the mathematical rigor of classical differential and variational calculus to obtain solutions to problems whose analytical properties are not completely known. If the analytical behavior of the objective function to be optimized is not known, it is possible, through experimentation, using some systematic search plan, to arrive at the optimal value of the function.

Many search techniques have been developed and used successfully in solving problems that could not be handled by classical methods. It is true that these procedures are heuristic and might be scorned by the mathematical purist, nevertheless, if used with the proper understanding of their limitations, they can be very effective in obtaining solutions.

Search methods can be classified as single- and multivariable cases. They can also be classified into simple search methods, in which no derivatives are computed, gradient methods, in which first derivatives of the objective function are used, and second-order methods, in which higher-order derivatives of the objective function are used. Because the nonlinearity, the large number of variables, and the inequality constraint features of the problem being studied require a search technique, this topic will be described in more detail following the general review of optimization techniques.

Common to all search methods is the general procedure used to derive the optimum value of the objective function. Changes in the independent variables of the system are made according to some strategy. The effects of these changes on the objective function are evaluated and the results of the evaluation are used to determine the next move. The process is iterative and is terminated when no further improvement on the objective function is possible. This section will discuss the forms of representation of the objective function, the main search strategies, and the problems and limitations of the search methods.

1. REPRESENTATION OF THE OBJECTIVE FUNCTION

Two methods are useful for representing the objective function. Although both are illustrated in terms of two variables, it is possible to extend this representation to n-dimensional space without much loss of insight. The first method, shown in Fig. 3.1, involves plotting the objective function $f(\bar{x})$ versus all the n independent variables in an $(n + 1)$-dimensional space. The second method, shown in Fig. 3.2, is a more useful form of representation. It is a family of loci of points with equal values of the objective function. Because these

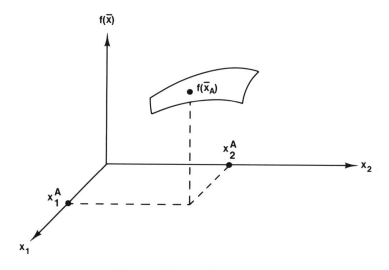

FIG. 3.1   Objective function surface.

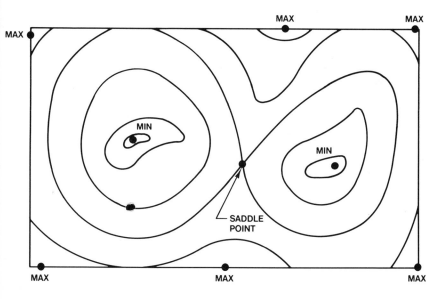

FIG. 3.2   Contour line map.

curves are analogous to the lines of equal elevation drawn on maps, they are called contour lines. Note in the figure the presence of two minima, a saddle point [a point where all derivatives vanish, but where $f(\bar{x} + \Delta x)$ could be either smaller or larger than $f(\bar{x})$], and several maxima, which all fall on the boundary of the region.

2. MULTIVARIABLE SEARCH

A great number of multivariable search techniques (with variations) are available. Only the most common methods and those required to give continuity to the development of the subject are mentioned here.

a. Single-Variable Adjustment Method

The single-variable adjustment method is the simplest search technique possible. Each parameter is changed individually until the objective function is minimized. The next parameter is then changed in the same way. The process is repeated until no further improvement in the objective function is possible. This method works for spherical contours but is extremely slow in general. Figure 3.3

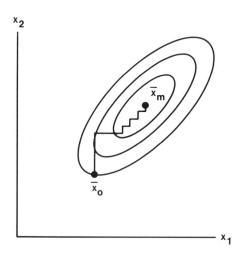

FIG. 3.3   Single-variable adjustment search method.

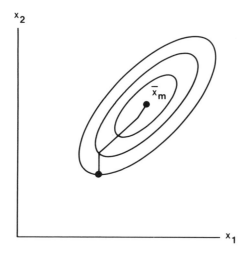

FIG. 3.4   Steepest descent method.

shows the path that this search method would take along a given contour map. A variation of this method, which sometimes converges faster, is to choose the direction of change randomly.

b. Steepest Descent Method

In the previous method, if a ridge is present that is not parallel to one of the axes, convergence will be very slow. As indicated earlier, a move in the direction of the gradient G (which is the direction of steepest descent) could eliminate this problem, as shown in Fig. 3.4.

c. General Parallel Tangent Method

The general parallel tangent (partan) method is an extension of the steep descent partan method, which does not make use of gradients. As shown in Fig. 3.5, given a point P_0 and the line π_0 tangent to the contour at that point, one can start at an arbitrary point P_2 and search along a line parallel to π_0. When the minimum point P_3 along that line is found, another search is initiated along the line $P_3 - P_0$. The minimum point is on that line. The general method in n-dimensional space alternates climbing with acceleration in such a way that the optimum can be found in no more than $2n - 1$ unidimensional searches and n contour tangent measurements.

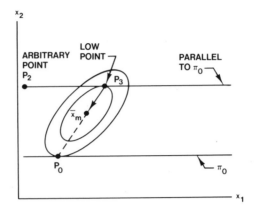

FIG. 3.5   General parallel tangent in two dimensions.

d. Pattern Search Method

This method is best suited for contours with sharp ridges, for which most of the other search methods are ineffective. The strategy used enables the crest of a ridge to be followed while searching for an optimum. It is based on the premise that any pattern of moves found successful during early experiments is worth trying again. Because of this property, straight ridges or boundaries are very easily followed using the pattern search technique.

e. Sequential Simplex Method

Sequential simplex is a very simple and ingenious method. For an n-parameter problem, one begins by choosing $n + 1$ points, which span the parameter space. If these points are connected, the resulting geometrical figure is called a *simplex,* hence the name of the method. The method involves tumbling and shrinking of this simplex toward the minimum in the following manner. First, the objective function is evaluated at each point. The point with the highest value is reflected about the center of gravity of the simplex. Then, if the value of the reflected point decreases, it is accepted and the process is repeated with the new set of points. On the other hand, if the reflected point has a higher value, the simplex is shrunk about the point with the lowest functional value. Expansion (analogous to acceleration for successful moves) and contraction can also be incorporated. This method is extremely easy to program but has the disadvantage that the simplex might contract into a subspace causing some directions of exploration to be permanently lost.

3. Limitations of Search Methods

Despite all the advantages of the search methods that have been discussed, there are some problems and limitations that must be appreciated to use these methods effectively. The first problem concerns the uniqueness of a minimum. Since search techniques operate on the principle of local excursion, the solutions found are only local minima. The assumption has been made that the objective functions under consideration are uninodal, that is, they have only one minimum in the allowed region. Only a systematic search over the entire parameter space can guarantee the uniqueness of a minimum. This is, of course, extremely impractical. A somewhat lesser guarantee of uniqueness can be obtained by repeating the optimization with a number of different starting points and observing whether each solution converges to the same minimum. Fortunately, in the optimization of an actual engineering system, finding any minimum (even if it is not a global minimum) is a satisfactory solution.

There are additional limitations. First, the nature of the function being optimized is such that a well-defined, smooth, objective hypersurface should be visualized. It is the representation of a physical system lacking discontinuities and other abnormal characteristics. Second, because the starting point is an actual operating point, it is already in the vicinity of the optimum point. Finally, the large number of constraints present restrict the solution space so much that it is very likely that the optimum point would be on one of the constraint boundaries rather than at a singular point. It should be pointed out, in conclusion, that the problem of local versus absolute extremum points is not unique to search methods but exists in classical analytical methods as well.

C. The Pattern Search Method

1. CRITERIA FOR SELECTING THE PATTERN SEARCH METHOD FOR OPTIMIZATION

The first question that must be answered is: What were the criteria used in selecting this method of optimization from all the others that have been described? The criteria used are itemized next.

a. *Ease of Implementation*

The pattern search method uses one of the simplest strategies of all methods described, yet, despite its simplicity, it is more effective than some of the more sophisticated strategies.

b. *Speed of Computation*

The inherent simplicity of the method makes the computational speed extremely high. Empirical observations of computation time indicate that it varies as the first power of the number of variables. This is striking when compared with the computation time for classical minimization techniques, which varies as the cube of the number of variables.

c. *Ability to Handle Inequality Constraints*

The problem being optimized involves inequality constraints, and thus the method used had to be able to handle them. As will be pointed out, a convenient way to handle these constraints with the pattern search method is to assign a penalty to the objective function. Thus the constraint boundaries effectively become ridges, which this method can follow well.

2. EXPLANATION OF THE PATTERN SEARCH STRATEGY

To illustrate the strategy used by the pattern search method, the path that would be followed in a given set of objective function contours is shown in Fig. 3.6. The strategy calls for two types of moves, exploratory and pattern. In exploratory moves, one variable at a time is adjusted by a step size that changes for each variable during the course of the search. A pattern move adjusts all variables in the direction established by the exploratory moves.

To develop a pattern, we start at the base point B_1 and make an explanatory move on x_1 to E_0. Since the value of the objective function increases, a move in the opposite direction is made to E_1. The x_2 variable is adjusted next. This establishes the next base point B_2. Note that, because of the success of the two exploratory moves, both step sizes have increased. A pattern has been established and

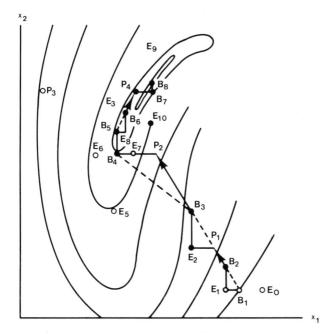

FIG. 3.6   Pattern search path. See text for details.

the next move is a pattern move to P_1 along the B_2B_1 vector. From P_1, two more exploratory moves are made to B_3. Another pattern move to P_2 is followed by an exploratory move in the $-x_1$ direction. Note that exploratory moves E_3 and E_5 both fail, thus B_4 is the next base point. The step in the x_2 direction is now decreased. Next, a pattern move is made to P_3. This move fails, leaving B_4 as the last base point. The exploration with reduced step sizes is continued establishing base points B_5, B_6, B_7, and B_8, which follow the ridge and locate the minimum. At each base point a pattern move is made, followed by an exploratory move using the previously established step size. Success causes the step size to be increased; failure decreases it. The process is terminated when all step sizes have been reduced to their minimum.

   Inequality constraints are handled by adding a penalty to the objective function any time one of the constraint boundaries is exceeded. This turns back any move that would violate a constraint boundary. In effect, the boundary becomes a ridge that the pattern search must follow.

D. Three Optimization Techniques Commonly Used in Energy Management Solutions

The three techniques discussed earlier in this chapter will now be detailed. Among many reasons for selecting these three methods in energy management system applications, the overriding considerations are availability of application software that can be easily tailored for the application on hand, ease with which the application software can handle the utility system constraints, and computational complexity of the application programs to yield useful optimization solutions quickly.

The three techniques to be expanded are linear programming, direct pattern search method (e.g., the Nelder–Mead Simplex method for functional minimization), and direct experimental search (e.g., unit cost allocation).

1. LINEAR PROGRAMMING

Linear programming is a viable approach to analyze and evaluate the decision variables (e.g., steam generation, kilowatts generated and/or purchased) in the utility plant that can be used for energy allocation and system planning. This technique has been applied in utility management, on both real-time and off-line simulation modes.

Figure 3.7 depicts a typical diagram of a steam plant with a material and energy balance. During normal operations, the demands for process steam and shaft horsepower may vary. Some of the shaft horsepower may be used to generate additional electrical power. Fluctuations may be due to shutdowns, new process demands, etc. When they occur, the production personnel must decide how to best meet the new demand. In general, these questions involve the trade-off of steam with electricity, or of the best level of operation of turbines with multiple exhaust and extraction options. The best solution is one that meets the demands at a minimum cost. The prob-

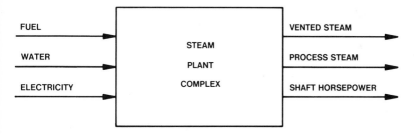

FIG. 3.7   Steam plant complex.

lem may be solved by standard linear programming techniques, with most of the constraints and the objective function approximated linearly.

a. *Plant Model*

The model is developed by assembling submodels of the various components in a plant's steam and electrical distribution system. Elements of the steam distribution system that are represented as variables in the model are boilers, flash tanks, pressure-reducing valves, desuperheating stations, deaerators, boiler feedwater heaters, and turbines. In addition, a number of constraints are placed on the model. These include material balances for each pressure of steam and for the condensate–feedwater system. In addition to these submodels, purchased fuel and power costs under the existing contracts must be introduced so that the impact of total energy cost can be evaluated as a function of utility demand variations and their peaks.

To form an integrated plant model, the submodels are connected to each other using mass and heat balances according to the actual plant configuration. Figure 3.8 represents a typical boiler operation, from which we develop a boiler submodel. Boilers consume fuel and convert feedwater to steam. Typically, a certain amount of the steam generation is lost to blowdown. The blowdown and flash steam affect the material balances, and thus the flash tank is represented as a part of the boiler. Similarly, to reduce the number of equations, boiler efficiency and fuel cost will be combined and represented as an entry in the objective function.

The boiler operation shown in Fig. 3.8 was computed for various values and is shown in Table 3.1. Table 3.1 shows the material

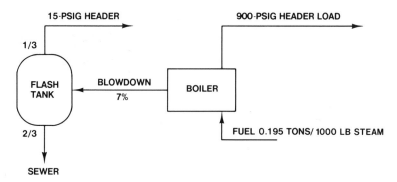

FIG. 3.8   Simplified boiler operation.

balance of the boiler and flash tank, including the cost of fuel based on 1000 lb of steam generation. This is the format used in linear programming technique in the solution for the decision variables that impact the utility operating costs.

b. *Validation of Model*

To validate the plant model and to match the plant operating conditions to that of the model, an initial test run should be made.

TABLE 3.1
Values of Boiler Plant Operation Shown in Fig. 3.8

Row	Boiler column	Explanation
Cost	0.192	(0.195 ton/1000 lb steam) × [fuel cost ($1/ton)] = $0.195/1000 lb. Assumes $1/ton cost in example.
Balance (psig)		
900	−1	Supply 1 lb 900-psig steam for every unit of activity in boiler column.
15	−0.0233	Supply 0.0233 lb 15-psig steam for every unit of activity in boiler column: 15 psig steam = 0.07 (0.333) = 0.0233 lb.
Feed water	1.07	Use 1.07 lb feedwater for every unit of activity in boiler column: Total feed = boiler + blowdown = boiler + 0.07 (boiler) = 1.07 (boiler).

TABLE 3.2
Model Validation and Optimum Settings

Parameter	Initial run	Match (M)	Optimum (O)	M − O
Steam generated (1000 lb/hr)	493.8	493.2	488.7	4.5
Variable cost ($/hr)	—	368	356	12
TG1 output (kV·A)	4.0	4.0	4.0	—
TG2 output (kV·A)	10.0	10.3	10.0	—
TG3 output (kV·A)	10.0	10.1	10.0	—
Total output (kV·A)	24.0	24.4	24.0	—

This is accomplished by imposing the plant "snap shot," the time-coincident meter readings, of the steam flows as appear in the steam balance. Table 3.2 is a typical example of a validation printout and includes the recommended levels of utility generations for optimum operation.

"Optimum" is the method of operation the model would have chosen if it were free to meet the demands in any way it could. "Initial run" shows some room for improvement, as the optimum operation requires 4.5 thousand pounds per hour less steam. This represents approximately 1% of the total steam generated. The percentage is small, and the limits of the model are approached when differentiating among various operating modes.

c. *Linear Programming Solution*

Once the plant model is formulated, the linear programming application software can be used to find the optimum total energy supply by solving for the minimum value of a linear function of several independent variables subject to linear constraints and/or inequalities. As a result of the optimization calculations, the solution yields optimum allocation of boiler and turbogenerator loads, target ranges for purchasing of kilowatts, optimum allocation of steam turbine versus motor drives, and optimum fuel dispatch.

The linear programming technique is a viable method for modeling utility generation and distribution systems. The greatest benefit of this approach is its ability to allow numerous cases on off-line simulation mode, enabling it to gain a good understanding of how a utility plant should be operated for maximum energy efficiency.

2. NELDER–MEAD: A SIMPLEX METHOD FOR FUNCTION MINIMIZATION (Nelder, 1967)

The Nelder–Mead method is used for the minimization of a function of n variables and depends on the comparison of function values at $n + 1$ vertices of a general simplex, followed by the replacement of the vertex with the highest value of another point.

The simplex adapts itself to the local landscape and contracts to the final minimum. The method is shown to be effective and computationally compact. The routine does not explicitly handle constraints, however, penalty functions have been used successfully with this routine. Generally, the number of functional evaluations required for convergence goes up roughly as the square of the number of variables.

The Nelder–Mead technique (as adapted for energy management applications) has been successfully installed in a number of industrial plants for optimum boiler load allocation and chiller optimization. One advantage of this program is that it tells the level to which each boiler or chiller must generate its load to satisfy a minimum cost for a given plant load. However, since the routine utilizes the utility model, it must be updated when it exceeds an acceptable bound. The boiler efficiency curve, as a function of the boiler load, is a variable in the calculation of the steam production cost. This technique also presents a problem because the efficiency curve must be recharacterized each time the fuel mix changes for multiple-fuel-firing boilers (Cho, 1978).

3. INDIVIDUAL UNIT COST ALLOCATION TECHNIQUE (Blevins, 1980)

Plant utility systems generally consist of multiple units of equipment operated in parallel producing utilities such as steam, electricity, chilled water, and compressed air. Basic analog control schemes consist of a master demand controller whose output is paralleled into the individual unit demand controls. This allows all units, as selected by the operator, to change load proportionally to satisfy the new demand.

The problem with this conventional parallel-demand control is that it is very difficult to take advantage of differences in efficiencies

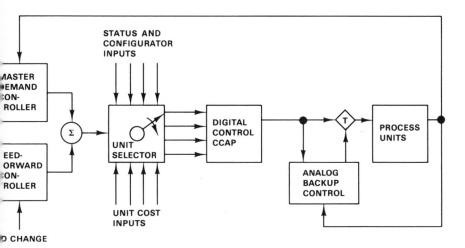

FIG. 3.9   Individual unit cost allocation technique using a minicomputer with analog backup. (From Blevins, 1980.)

or costs of producing the utility on the parallel units that are not base-loaded. A better approach would be for the unit with the lowest current cost of producing a unit of the utility to produce that unit when an increase in that utility is required. Likewise, the unit with the highest cost of producing a unit of the utility would reduce production using the individual unit cost allocation (IUCA).

Figure 3.9 represents a typical implementation of the IUCA technique using a minicomputer with an analog backup. The control scheme in the computer is implemented using the energy management calculations package (EMCP) and the energy optimization package (EOP) as well as the standard continuous control application program (CCAP). The three major functions performed in the computer are configuration, control–unit selection and unit cost calculation and organization.

a. *Configuration*

Configuration determines which units are available for allocation by the control. The function of the configuration operation is shown in Fig. 3.10. The availability of a unit is determined by the two status flags L_N and L_M. The flag L_N is set to indicate that a minimum constraint has been reached and the load on the unit cannot be

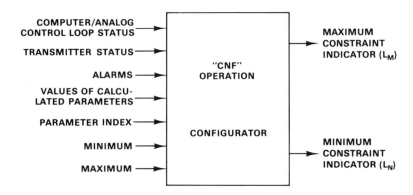

FIG. 3.10   Configuration function.

reduced further by the allocation. The flag L_M is set to indicate that a maximum constraint has been reached and the load cannot be increased. If both flags are set, the load on the unit cannot be changed. There are three minimum–maximum type status checks performed by the configuration function (CNF) and four absolute status inputs.

The absolute status inputs for the CNF can be calculated in the EMCP using the extensive logic calculations available. The conditions that might be considered in the status calculations are computer interface equipment status, computer and/or analog control loop status, transmitter status, alarms, and values of calculated parameters. The status outputs from the configurator operation are inputs to the unit selection (US) function in the IUCA control path.

A discrete control function is another part of the configuration procedure. This function monitors internal and external conditions and regulates discrete outputs that can transfer the unit control to backup analog should particular conditions occur.

b. *Unit Cost Calculation and Organization*

The unit cost calculation and organization constitute the other support path to the IUCA control. The allocation objective (unit costs) are calculated through operations in the EMCP. This allows customization for the particular application. It is then the function of the unit cost organizer (UCO) operation to arrange unit numbers into a unit allocation array in the order of ascending or descending values of unit costs. An example of the rearrangement of unit cost

UNIT COST DATA

UNIT NO.	1	2	3	4	5	6	7	8	9
COST	2.9	2.3	2.8	2.5	2.1	2.6	2.2	2.7	2.4

UNIT ALLOCATION ARRAY

PRIORITY	1	2	3	4	5	6	7	8	9
UNIT NO.	5	7	2	9	4	6	8	3	1

LOWEST   HIGHEST

FIG. 3.11   Unit cost and unit allocation array format.

data into a unit cost array is represented in Fig. 3.11. This unit allocation array is used by the US function in the IUCA control path.

c. *Control/Unit Selection*

The control path of the IUCA technique starts with a master demand controller (MDC). The controller has as its input the process variable used as the feedback indication of utility demand. Either the standard proportional plus integral plus derivative (PID) function in CCAP or a special controller, the MDC function, can be used. The MDC adds the capability to have independent PID tuning constants for each unit in the allocation. The tuning constants are selected based on feedback from the US function. Before and after the controller function, standard CCAP functions can be used. Figure 3.9 shows a summer after the demand controller that incorporates a feedforward load signal.

The combined feedback–feedforward demand signal transmitted to the US function must be a differential signal. This is because the US function, which is the heart of the IUCA technique, monitors the sign of the load input signal and determines which unit or units should handle the requested load change. The decision is based on status information from the CNF, unit cost data in the unit allocation array, maximum and minimum unit load changes and unit load maximum and minimum set points. The last two items are the means by which a load change can be distributed to more than one unit at a time. Should the load change exceed the available capacity, a message indicating this situation is printed for the operator.

The outputs from the US are set points for CCAP control loops. Each unit has a particular control loop associated with it, which is specified in the unit's database.

d. *Applications*

The IUCA technique can be applied to perform control and optimization for many different applications. These applications include boiler and turbogenerator load allocation, multifuel boiler fuel optimization, allocation of secondary fuels on boiler, turbogenerator extraction flow allocation, turbogenerator tie-line control, and chiller and air compressor load allocations.

Because the IUCA technique is a sophisticated digital controller, its characteristics are those of a controller. When activated by the operator, it is initialized to the current operating conditions. The US then decouples the regulation of load between units and chooses the most efficient one to increase or decrease the total utility load. The control actions move the units to an optimum load configuration and keep the units optimally loaded. Because the technique requires control actions to drive the optimization, the units will be moved only as a result of natural changes in demand. This prevents artificial changes in unit demands being imposed on the system. This technique also allows for consistent maintenance of the units at optimum loads.

4

Selecting Computer Systems

There are a number of ways for the project manager to select a computer system for an energy management project. Either the in-house project team or an outside engineering consultant should develop a specification that clearly outlines and describes the system requirements. This specification is then distributed among qualified manufacturers of hardware and system engineering services, who submit price quotes on the project.

It may be necessary for key plant personnel in the project team to interview and evaluate the capability of manufacturers by visiting their plant. This allows the project team members to select suppliers who are not only capable of supplying state-of-the-art equipment, but who have experienced project managers, systems engineers, and service personnel to handle all phases of project implementation and

57

startup. If the buyer already has a list of qualified manufacturers, then the specifications for quotation are distributed among those selected.

The process of selecting a computer system and other complementing instruments and equipment is the single most important phase of any successful computer-based project. This chapter will be developed with emphasis on the needs of users and suppliers. Specifications will be given covering all aspects of computer system selection.

A. General Philosophy of Selecting a Computer System

When designing and purchasing a process computer system, a logical strategy should be followed so that the final selection will both meet the process requirements and be cost-effective. This section will define the various steps in the selection strategy and will provide some guidance by identifying possible pitfalls.

To specify and select a computer system, the buyer's strategy should consist of four steps: the definition of process control and management requirements; the definition of software functions necessary to satisfy the requirements; the determination of the size of the main memory, auxiliary storage, and processing speed required by the estimated size of the software; and the selection of a minicomputer or microprocessor-based computer system and the necessary peripherals.

Figure 4.1 is a flowchart that defines the tasks necessary for the selection of a microprocessor-based energy management system or any process-control system.

One problem with this method is that there is usually a wide price range for hardware items having approximately the same performance. Therefore, hardware selection should not be based on cost alone. Other considerations, e.g., reliability and compatibility with other system components, also have a significant influence on the success of the project.

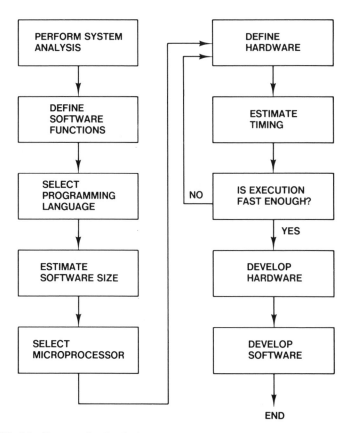

FIG. 4.1   Strategy for developing a process control system. (From U.S. Department of Energy, 1979.)

1. SYSTEM ANALYSIS

Once the project goals are defined, the next step is to perform a detailed analysis of the process to be controlled. This should include a survey of all variables to be monitored or controlled and a block diagram of the process. This block diagram shows the approximate locations of the various signal transmitters and final control elements and their distances from the central control room.

The preliminary system analysis should provide information about control variables, specifying the number of inputs (e.g., flow, temperature, level, and contact switches) and the types of signals (e.g., voltages and current). It should also include information about manipulated variables, such as the number of outputs (e.g., output to controllers and motor starters) and the types of signals (e.g., current, pulses, and voltages).

The lists of process variable information require both inputs and outputs to configure a system. This information will be especially useful during the software development phase of the project.

The controlled variable information should include engineering units, processing frequency (scans per second), maximum, minimum, and alarm limits, maximum allowable deviation from set point, and set point.

For the manipulated variable, necessary information includes engineering units, maximum adjustment per pass, and minimum and maximum time between adjustments.

2. DEFINE SOFTWARE FUNCTIONS

The specific software-controlled functions of the computer are determined by the process requirements. Some possible functions and the associated software are data logging and monitoring, control, and analysis.

Data logging and monitoring consist of variable scanning, averaging, and storing, data file management, report generating, limit checking, and alarming.

The control function includes controller tuning (through standard PID action) and process modeling.

The analysis function comprises variable plotting and data regression.

3. SELECT A PROGRAMMING LANGUAGE

It is necessary to select a programming language only for a newly developed system. Most computer control systems made by original equipment manufacturers are preprogrammed for a specific application and are usually equipped with a custom software package. When developing a new system, however, the selection of the programming language will have a great impact on the total development costs. In fact, as stated previously, software development usually accounts for the greater part of the overall costs.

The choice of a programming language for a microcomputer is limited to some extent, but the manufacturers of the more popular microcomputers usually make available a high-level language other than the assembly language. When selecting a programming language, one must consider the programming proficiency of the support staff, the availability of development aids for the particular language chosen (e.g., cross-compilers, cross-assemblers, emulators, syntax checkers, and simulators), the additional memory and peripherals necessary if an assembler or compiler is resident, and future program maintenance.

Usually, the most difficult choice is whether to write the application programs in a high-level or assembly language. Both have advantages. Programs coded in a high-level language are easier to write and maintain, but an assembly language usually leads to more efficient use of the computer's resources such as memory.

The best programming language combination seems to be as follows:

(1) *microcode* for frequently used routines, such as arithmetic functions, because microcode runs four times faster than assembly machine language;
(2) *assembly* machine language for fast memory access and real-time I/O interface control (peripheral drivers, system routines, etc.);
(3) *high level* for mathematical and logical manipulations and control algorithms, where development costs are usually high.

4. ESTIMATE SOFTWARE SIZE

The next step is to estimate the total software size in bytes. This includes software for control support and auxiliary functions as well as any additional development or system software required.

To define the main memory and auxiliary storage requirements, software should be classified as resident and nonresident. Resident software directs the critical functions of the system, remaining in execution almost all the time. It should include the scanning, alarming, and controlling functions. Nonresident software resides in the auxiliary storage (disk or tape) and performs the noncritical functions such as report generating and plotting.

5. SELECT MICROPROCESSOR

Eight and sixteen bits are the two most popular word lengths used in process control. The newer 16-bit microprocessors have several attractive features. These include more powerful instruction sets, faster processing rates than the 8-bit chip, simplified programming and the ability to handle 8- as well as 16-bit instructions.

Once the word size is selected, one must next select a manufacturer. Even though the word lengths are the same, each microprocessor has its own unique instruction set. Some may be easier to program than others. Some lend themselves more to the transferring of data, but others are more suitable for programming computational algorithms. In any case, making the correct selection has a significant impact on subsequent hardware and software development costs.

6. DEFINE HARDWARE REQUIREMENTS

Hardware requirements are determined by the process requirements. The type of hardware used affects the operating speed and efficiency of the microcomputer, therefore the appropriate hardware must be chosen carefully. The basic microcomputer, other than the microprocessor, consists of a real-time clock, memory, and interface.

At this point, memory type and size can be estimated, but the exact requirements will not be known until the control algorithms and other programs are written. Control and data-acquisition routines that remain unchanged are usually stored in ROM, PROM, or EPROM. Collected process information is temporarily stored in RAM while it is averaged or filtered. RAM is volatile and may be static or dynamic. Dynamic RAM costs less than static RAM, but it can hold data for only a few milliseconds. Thus it must be continuously refreshed (the contents of the memory rewritten), and refreshing usually requires some external refresh hardware.

The number of I/O ports and interfaces depends on the type and number of inputs, outputs, and peripheral devices. The I/O interfaces are either serial or parallel. Parallel interfaces are used to transfer data between the microprocessor and fast I/O devices such as disks. Serial interfaces are used with slower I/O devices such as teletypes.

In process-control applications, analog-to-digital and digital-to-analog converters are usually necessary. Most process signals, such as temperature and pressure, are continuous or analog and as such must be converted to digital form. Likewise, some computer outputs (for example, the signal to the current-to-pressure transducer in most control valves) must be converted from digital to analog.

The peripheral devices are also defined by the primary function of the microcomputer and by whether or not the microcomputer will be supervised by a central host. For example, if the microcomputer is a stand-alone system monitoring and controlling a process, it should be equipped with a CRT and disk for data entry and storage. If it is a dedicated controller supervised by another micro- or minicomputer, it can temporarily store the process data in RAM where it can be accessed by the supervisor every few minutes.

Other hardware devices that should be considered are power-failure protection to prevent losing the temporary process data stored in RAM, automatic restart, floating-point arithmetic, direct memory access, and hardware interrupt.

At this point, it should be determined whether the combined hardware-software design is fast enough to carry out program execution in real time? If not, both the hardware and software should be re-evaluated.

7. DEVELOP SOFTWARE

After the hardware has been developed or purchased, the program must be written. This is the most expensive phase of the development effort. Software development costs for some microprocessor systems have been reported to be as high as $10 per line of debugged code.

There are four major options in microprocessor software development, but not all may be practical. Special microcomputer development systems are available for some microprocessors or software may be cross-assembled, cross-compiled, or simulated through time-sharing networks. Microprocessor resident development software is another option, as is hand assembly.

Microcomputer software development systems are usually available for lease from the manufacturers of complete systems during the software development phase of a new system. Applications programs can also be developed through some of the national time-sharing services. These cross-assemblers, compilers, and simulators are generally written in FORTRAN.

The first step is to cross-assemble or compile the program logic. The output is usually in the form of object code. Depending on the time-sharing service, this output may be on punched paper tape or on a ROM chip. In either case, it is generally very well documented. Software development through time-sharing is probably the most expensive option, but it has many advantages.

Resident assemblers and compilers are not as powerful and do not provide the documentation available through cross-assemblers and cross-compilers. In addition, the microcomputer must be off-line while the program is being developed. However, all this may be offset by a much lower development cost. Hand assembly is by far the most tedious and impractical method, nevertheless it is used quite extensively. Hand assembly involves writing a program to change mnemonics to machine language. This method is obviously time consuming and is not recommended for programs that contain more than 200 instructions.

8. BEWARE OF THE PITFALLS

Although developing the hardware for a specific application will yield a system more readily adapted to one's application than a purchased system, the development costs are much greater.

There are many trade-offs to be considered. For example, let us consider whether to program in an assembly or a high-level language. For a typical microcomputer system, programs written in a high-level language require between 1.5 and 5 times as much memory as programs written in assembly language, but they take only half as long to develop. Thus a trade-off exists between the cost of additional memory and the cost of programming time.

B. A Typical System Specification Generated by a User

The major elements governing a computer specification are supplier and shipping requirements, energy management system requirements, and testing and inspection. The specification should contain general information, and be able to satisfy the specific requirements pertaining to the project at hand as it relates to the process control objectives and goals. There is a logical step by which the project team can arrive at a final selection of the computer system which consists of carefully evaluating the bidders' responses to the specification.

1. SUPPLIER REQUIREMENTS

In this section will be discussed the information related to project type, location, and site conditions. It is also important to confirm the compatibility of the system with the process operations and with any standard to which the system design must conform, such as the National Fire Protection Association (NFPA) Standard.

The supplier's responsibility as related to project management must be clearly spelled out. It must be determined whether the project is to be a turnkey or whether the areas of project responsibility and management are to be distributed between the supplier and the user.

a. *Process Descriptions and Management Objectives*

i. Boilers

The system should optimize the operation of existing and future boilers in converting available fuels to 800-psi pressure heaters. The boiler data are

(1) 250,000 lb/hr gas and oil package,
(2) 300,000 lb/hr pulverized coal and gas ignition,
(3) 400,000 lb/hr pulverized coal and gas ignition, and
(4) a future boiler with 400,000 lb/hr pulverized coal and gas ignition.

For all the boilers the computer should include an exit flue-gas analysis of O_2, opacity, NO_x, and combustibles (CO) as well as an automatic O_2 trim.

The computer system should calculate and log the efficiency of all the boilers using ASME power test codes: heat loss and I/O method. It should also, on demand, display the boiler operating parameters, for example, excess air, excess gas temperature, combustion air temperature, draft loss, kilowatt consumption, and steam temperature.

The computer should allocate loads to boilers so that a minimum steam production cost can be realized. Steam data concerning each boiler should be provided for Btu's added per pound of steam made and cost per pound of steam made.

ii. Turbogenerators

The system should maximize the conversion of 800-psi steam for cogeneration. The turbogenerators have 30-MW, 100-lb extraction, 20-lb back pressure and a 50-MW, 100-lb extraction, 20-lb back-pressure condensing unit. Provisions should also be made for at least two additional turbine generators.

The computer should optimize operation of turbogenerators to obtain maximum by-product kilowatts. Control of the generator excitation system should be in conjuction with utility tie control.

Calculations should be made of the actual kilowatt cost for 100-lb by-product kilowatts, 20-lb by-product kilowatts, and condensing kilowatts. The computer should monitor all electrical loads in connection with condensing kilowatts, mainly the loads of pumps and cooling tower fans.

iii. Tie-Line Control

To minimize electrical power costs the system should operate in conjunction with the local utility company through the tie-line. The computer should purchase power based on the ratio between purchased and condensed kilowatts. It should also purchase power to stay within contract limits at minimum cost.

The system should operate in conjunction with power generation to maintain the maximum reactive power from the utility without penalty. When deciding whether to make or buy power the system should include a feasibility plan for the purchase of off-peak power.

iv. Electrical Load Shedding

The load-shedding program should include ten possible sheddable loads. The load shed/restore program should interact with loss of electrical generation, loss of utility tie-line, and power-demand control strategy.

2. ENERGY MANAGEMENT SYSTEM REQUIREMENTS

The system should be microprocessor-based and connected via a digital data highway to multiple CRT operator stations. Control functions should be user-configurable to perform specific control strategies.

The system should include control cabinets, as required, to contain the necessary controllers and support hardware, control system I/O units, termination cabinets for wiring I/O's to field devices, and peripheral devices as required, including, but not limited to, a video copier and printer. The system should be designed so that major portions of it will not be shut down by the failure of any single device.

The controllers may be single- or multiloop microprocessors with algorithms selected from the console. In the event of microprocessor controller failures, these stations should have the capability to manually manipulate the control device. The system should employ preconfigured-process control algorithms and provide flexibility for completely configuring the system without the need for software programming.

a. *Hardware Functions*

Configurable controllers should have a standard PID control function with bumpless, balanceless transfer from automatic to manual and from manual to automatic.

Many functions should also be available to provide capability or control system configuration. They should include, but not be limited to, lead–lag, high and low selectors, summer, multiplier, divider, auto–manual, integrator–totalizer, ratio, process indicator, and function generator. A configurable controller should also have signal conditioning and contact/logic functions.

b. *Security of the System*

Devices within the system must be under continuous surveillance by diagnostic programs. The controllers should include internal self-checks and status indications.

Controllers having volatile memories should be protected by backup power. The station should have memory backup in the form of a floppy disk that can be loaded back into the system should a power failure occur. The memory backup should include the database and control configurations.

Partitioning of control functions among multifunction microprocessors should be designed so that the failure of a single microprocessor module does not cause interruption or loss of control of more than a single subsystem.

c. *Data Communications*

The communications subsystem should be a redundant digital highway that provides a data path among all controllers, I/O devices, the operator interface, the computer, and other highway devices.

Communications security should include the following minimum requirements:

(1) continuous on-line monitoring and reporting of the status of both the primary and redundant data highway and all connected devices,
(2) error checks on all data transfers,
(3) automatic retries in the event of errors, and
(4) system-level fault diagnosis.

d. *CRT Consoles*

CRT consoles should be located in an environmentally controlled room that has a general-purpose, nonhazardous electrical area classification. The consoles will display all relevant information and control functions. Certain basic functions should be provided at the operator console. These include an indication of controlled and non-controlled process variables, database and configuration formats, manipulation of control loops (set point, control modes, output), manipulation of alarm settings, trend recording, alarm annunciation, display, and acknowledgment, and logging of alarms and operator control changes on the printer.

A keylock provision would permit the engineer to change tuning constants, process variable zero and span values, alarm limits, and loop configuration.

e. *Alarms*

The alarm monitoring system should be capable of detecting off-normal conditions within the control system and recognizing off-normal conditions generated by field-mounted dry contacts. The operator's console should be capable of displaying alarms for any loop in the system.

Alarms should be included to detect process variable high, low, low–low, or high–high, deviation from set point, deviation of output from a predetermined value, deviation of set point from a predetermined value, high or low, and rate of change. Diagnostic alarms should also be included.

The alarm display function should use an alarm message format and update a selected CRT when a point is in alarm status. The occurence of an alarm shall alert the operator by means of an audible sound as well as a flashing, video, or color change condition on the CRT and/or operator keyboard. Means should be provided to inform the operator of the page location of the alarm.

Upon acknowledgement of an alarm, the audible sound should be silenced and the flashing should stop. However, a means should be provided to indicate that the value is still in alarm condition. The alarm is cleared when the condition returns to normal.

f. *Operator CRT Display*

Each operator CRT and keyboard should, as a minimum, have overview, group, and detail display.

g. *Input Data*

An analog, digital, and manual input list should be provided for both control and non-control process variables and status types. Thus the system can be sized to handle inputs and process them for the energy management system.

h. *Power Requirement*

Plant availability and supplier responsibility for power source, power supply, power distribution, and ground bus requirements must be clearly stated.

i. *Cabinets*

The need for system cabinets and I/O or termination cabinets (including all wiring) should be clearly specified.

3. TESTING AND INSPECTION

The entire system should be staged and given a complete factory test prior to shipment. The buyer should perform a complete acceptance test of the system at the factory site to his or the project team's satisfaction. A process simulation may be necessary to evaluate the validity of the system functional test.

After installation of the system at the plant site, a field test should be performed to verify the proper operation of the system. Normally, start-up assistance is included in the purchase contract.

4. SHIPMENT REQUIREMENTS

Packaging and shipping instructions should be clearly communicated to the supplier to prevent contamination and mechanical damage. It is important that all interconnecting cables are labeled at each end, specifying the cabinet, terminal panel, or plug-in receptable to which it is to be reconnected.

5. OTHER PROVISIONS

Exceptions to the specifications or alternative solutions must be clearly stated so that the buyer can review the acceptability of the system as quoted. The seller should provide system installation, maintenance, operating instructional manuals, and a list of recommended spare parts. The seller should also provide training courses for both engineers and technicians.

C. A Typical Quotation Generated by a Supplier

The supplier, in response to the specification, generates a quotation that specifies the costs for hardware, software, and support services.

1. HARDWARE

The hardware for the computer energy management system should include a custom computer, operator's and engineer's consoles, traffic director, and primary, and data highways, controllers, multiplexers, a trend unit, and a line printer.

2. SOFTWARE

Software changes can be divided into utility programs and custom software. Utility programs are prewritten programs that provide the nucleus of instructions needed for such tasks as configuration, display building, and database management. Custom software are programs that are specially designed and tailored for the computer functions defined in the specifications. For the specification prescribed in Section A, the following software is supplied: boiler optimization calculations, boiler efficiency calculations, turbogenerator efficiency calculations, turbogenerator allocation calculations, utility tie-line control, and electrical load shedding.

3. SUPPORT SERVICES

The elements of a support service are system services, start-up services, and system consultation. These services are usually quoted for estimated manweeks or per diem plus expenses. System services include database definition, display building, and project management.

System consultation involves the development of control strategies and recommendation of system optimization for the user. Start-up services should include software for boilers, turbogenerators, tie-line control, and electric load shedding. Start-up hardware service should provide installation supervision, start-up assistance, trouble-shooting, and on-site training.

D. Software Specification

Once the user has selected a supplier, the supplier develops, with user participation, a detailed software specification. The software specification becomes a base document that defines the end product.
The software specification should include the following elements.

(1) *Introduction:*
    (a) system description,
    (b) scope of specification,
    (c) organization of specification, and
    (d) hardware block diagram.
(2) *I/O data:*
    (a) analog signals,
    (b) digital signals, and
    (c) manual signals.
(3) *Memory:*
    (a) general description and
    (b) bulk memory general description.
(4) *Peripheral units:*
    (a) peripheral unit interface,
    (b) line printer, and
    (c) CRT consoles.
(5) *System softwares:*
    (a) scope,
    (b) utility program, and
    (c) custom software.
(6) *System description:*
    (a) function diagram,
    (b) displays,
    (c) logs,
    (d) defined requests, and
    (e) messages.

(7) *System implementation and acceptance:*
  (a) scope,
  (b) general schedule,
  (c) factory hardware acceptance,
  (d) system acceptance,
  (e) system startup,
  (f) operator training,
  (g) system documentation, and
  (h) software support.

E. Systems Engineering Services Available from Manufacturers

During the preliminary phase of the computer selection process, it is important to ascertain which system engineering services are available from the manufacturers. A systems engineering checklist, such as the one shown in this section, helps to further define the elements that must be considered in the implementation of a successful computer project.

The systems engineering services should be evaluated to determine how the project is to be managed by the selected manufacturer and what the appropriate services are for the plant to contract from a manufacturer. Obviously, the need for systems engineering services is entirely dependent on the in-house capabilities and manpower availability.

1. PROJECT MANAGEMENT SERVICES

The project manager is responsible for the interdepartmental coordination of the technical and administrative activities required to provide a control system as specified in the purchase order. The factory project manager is the only person with the authority to commit resources and make decisions affecting system price, delivery, or performance. There is also a need for a person with similar authority at the user organization.

a. *Basic System Project Management*

The basic system project management defines the project management services provided with every system order. This service applies only to the standard hardware content of the system. The project manager oversees the project during its manufacturing and staging cycle and through the standard acceptance test and billing.

b. *Custom System Project Management*

Custom system project management is provided when the purchase order includes such items as buyout hardware, systems engineering services, special staging, and generation of special progress reports. These items have project management requirements that go beyond those provided in basic system project management.

On such projects, the project manager must direct the process of interpreting the user requirements and producing the project specification. This specification details the work that will be performed by the supplier in the execution of the purchase order. Once the project specification is approved and signed by the customer, the project manager maintains strict adherence to it and resolves problems during the implementation and start-up phases.

2. PROJECT SCOPE AND EVALUATION

a. *Control Study*

A control study is an analysis of current or proposed process operations to determine the opportunities and justification for improved process control. The result of a control study may include recommendations for a generic process control system, process control strategies depicted via process–instrument diagrams, and a cost–benefit analysis based on satisfying the recommendations with a control system.

b. *Plant Instrumentation Survey*

A plant instrumentation survey is an analysis of the objectives of a prospective process control system to determine the instrumentation requirements. The results of a plant instrumentation survey may include control system bill of material to satisfy the objectives and recommendations where appropriate.

c. *Consultation Services*

Consultation services are assistance that can be provided to the user on any aspect of the control system project. It is typically provided when another party has responsibility for a facet of the project but desires support because of a lack of familiarity with a given item.

These services can have a very narrow scope; they might consist of answering questions on how to use a controller function or manipulate a math function in a console. They can also be very broad, for instance, helping to design some of the control strategies, giving special schools to the people responsible for engineering the project, or determining the best approach for adding to an existing control system. This is a flexible service and the outcome is dependent on the specific work provided.

d. *Special Application Software Evaluation*

Once the decision has been made to use a computer with nonstandard functionality in the control room (e.g., interfacing another computer system to the main system), an evaluation is necessary. This begins with an evaluation of the conceptual design of the major software modules and an identification of the computer hardware required.

The next step is the analysis of the anticipated performance of the software in the computer hardware and in the overall control system.

The results are estimates of system loading, execution speeds, memory allocation, etc. Although these estimates are not exact and do not guarantee that the proposed hardware and software will yield the desired functionality, they are a necessary first-round check. The estimates are in the form of diagrams, hardware bills of material, and written text that constitute the input to the special computer software definition work.

3. PROJECT SCOPE AND SPECIFICATION

a. *Project Specification*

The detailed functional design work is performed in the project scope and specification phase. The following sections identify the areas of work and explain the design and definition work that takes place in each one. The results of this phase are written text, hardware lists, and diagrams.

Once the project specification is completed, detailed project schedule information is added and sent to the user for review. A meeting is held to answer technical and commercial questions, address disagreements, and achieve a document to which both parties agree. If any modifications are incorporated in the project specification, it is signed by both parties and constitutes the exact definition to work to be performed by the supplier. Any subsequent changes in system hardware or desired functionality are accompanied by a review to determine if any hardware or service pricing adjustments are necessary.

When the project specification is signed, the implementation phase can begin. This is the phase in which hardware is procured, system software developed, and services performed.

b. Control-System Hardware

i. Hardware Specification Sheet Preparation

Hardware specification sheets define the console and cabinet hardware and physical arrangement. Special care should be taken when preparing the specification sheets to assure that the configuration engineering will match and run successfully in the specified hardware.

ii. Power and Grounding System Design Consultation

It is the user's responsibility to assure that the primary and (if required) the backup ac power and grounding provided for the system will meet the system requirements. If uncertainty exists or problems are anticipated, professional assistance should be sought to define the required power and grounding. Power and grounding system designers analyze and recommend protective measures for transient disturbances, over-voltages, under-voltages, and loss of power.

iii. Environmental Review

The responsibility for assuring that the control system hardware successfully operates in the installed environment lies solely with the user. If uncertainty exists about the suitability of that environment, the user should seek professional assistance to establish an environmental specification.

If specific requirements are given, protective measures for excessive temperature, humidity, electromagnetic interference, vibration, and gaseous or particulate contaminates may be recommended. Typically, these protective measures will identify special cabinet and enclosure requirements for housing the control system hardware. Equipment selection in the control room layout and cabinet console layout will be governed by those environmental enclosure recommendations.

iv. Control-Room Layout

The control-room layout is the overall design and organization of the control room and any other operator interface locations. Placement of major pieces of equipment such as operator's and engineer's consoles, control panels, and equipment cabinets is determined by the availability of floor space, maintenance and operating clearances, power and signal access, and ergonomic considerations.

v. Cabinet and Console Layout

Cabinet and console drawings show the arrangement and dimensions of cabinets and consoles in the control room.

vi. Panel Layout

Panel layout is the overall design and organization of a control panel. Placement of indicating instruments, operator interface stations, enunciator panels, chart recorders, switches, etc., is based on physical and ergonomic considerations. Design drawings should include panel layout or, if the complete panel is to be provided, dimensional drawings should be supplied.

vii. Buyout Specification

Any control system device that is not in the supplier's price book is considered a buyout item and requires special attention in the specification, procurement, and staging phases. Some examples of buyout items are special cabinets for rack or console equipment, minicomputer equipment, intrinsic safety barriers, and programmable logic controller (PLC) equipment.

Buyout specification is the identification of the exact hardware configuration required to satisfy process requirements and to be electronically, mechanically, and functionally compatible with the control system. The specification contains information necessary for making the selection and specifying the equipment to be purchased. The equipment can be integrated into the system by the user and checked out at the staging site or at a location determined by the user.

viii. Spares Determination

Spares determination is the identification of the additional control system hardware to be purchased by the customer for start-up and ongoing system maintenance. The amount and type of spare equipment depend on the customer's desired maintenance philosophy.

4. CONTROL SYSTEM SERVICES

a. *Control Definition*

Control definition describes the control strategies required for the system to achieve the results specified by the control study. The result of the control definition is a document containing process–instrument diagrams and written descriptions to clarify complex control strategies. For the diagrams to be considered complete, they must include information about all mode logic (other than standard), tracking signals and logic, controller type, all inputs and input channel numbers, and all outputs and output channel numbers.

Another type of control definition work is the development of algorithms for process simulation. This simulation will typically be used for dynamic operator training or special system testing. Process simulation work usually consists of analysis of the process to determine the dynamic characteristics of control system inputs and the relationship between them, development of a mathematical model to approximate the above, and implementation of the model in the control system.

The typical form of implementation is the development of configuration software for the digital controllers. When process simulation is started, the configuration software will be downloaded into the controllers that are hardwired (or softwired) into the controllers having the control strategies.

b. *Process I/O Definition*

The process I/O point definition consists of an assemblage of the basic information required for each point in the system. The result of the process I/O definition is a spread sheet that contains the following information for each control system input or output:

(1) point tag,
(2) point descriptor,
(3) point type,
(4) point source,
(5) engineering units (EU) (analog points),
(6) EU high-conversion factor (analog points),
(7) EU low-conversion factor (analog points),
(8) high alarm value (analog points),
(9) low alarm value (analog points),
(10) deviation alarm value (analog points),
(11) on/alarm set point (discrete points),
(12) off/normal set point (discrete points),
(13) increase open/close action (output to field equipment),
(14) signal filter requirements (analog points) such as filter time constant,
(15) linearization requirements (nonlinear transmitter) such as square root and thermocouple types,
(16) transmitter calibration for pressure–temperature compensation, and
(17) display status, which may be one or more of the following: ND (not displayed), CD (control display), GD (graphics display), TR (trend), and AC (accumulate).

c. *Operator Interface Definition*

The operator interface definition is the design of how the operator will interface with the control system. A written configuration guideline for console configuration software development should be produced, with the user concurrence, to the specific needs of the control system and plant operations personnel. These guidelines include display philosophy, display hierarchy, optimal use of color schemes, and individual display formats. Once the guideline has been finalized and is mutually agreed to, it will be followed in the design and implementation of the operator console displays.

The final function of the operator interface definition is the development of a list of job-extended considerations (items that take exception to or are not covered by the customized guidelines).

d. *Special Computer Software Specification*

Special computer software specification takes the concept design work from the special application software evaluation phase and performs the next level of detailed design. This effort defines how the special software should be designed to accomplish the functionality of the conceptual design. The specific operational characteristics, constraints, expandability, and data requirements will be identified.

Another round of estimates for system loading, execution speeds, and memory allocation is done. While the complete and exact figures will not be known until the computer is programmed, tested, and operational, this second-round estimation will yield a higher level of precision than the estimates from the special computer software evaluation.

The result is a written report consisting of text and diagrams and is included in the project specification. Once the specification is reviewed and accepted by the user, the detailed programming and test phase is ready to begin.

e. *Special Acceptance Test and Staging Definition*

The special acceptance test and staging define any additional assembly checkout or system function demonstration beyond the normal staging and acceptance testing activities required for acceptance by the customer. Typical examples are the integration, testing, and demonstration of buyout hardware, special computer software, configuration software, interfile or special wiring, and special testing.

In cases where the user wishes to verify the control strategies, process simulation software may be developed for that purpose. The result is a section in the specification that defines all system functions to be tested, the methods and procedures to be used by staging personnel, and the actual checklist to be used during demonstration to the customer.

f. *Special Training*

Special training is any training beyond that offered in the supplier's standard educational center. An example is a school where operators are familiarized with the particular displays and control strategies prepared for their system. This type of school can use static displays or process simulation to give the operators experience in a dynamic setting similar to the process they will be controlling.

g. *Start-up Services Definition*

The definition of start-up services determines who is responsible for the site preparation, installation, commissioning, start-up, and final acceptance criteria of the system. The primary result is a section in the project specification that defines the criteria and checklist for final system acceptance by the user.

5. PROJECT IMPLEMENTATION

a. *Configuration Software Engineering*

Configuration software engineering translates the design work and process and control system information of the process I/O definition, control definition, operator interface definition, and hardware specification sheet sections into configuration software worksheets used in the configuration software entry phase. These worksheets are the standard ones provided in the documentation package.

The control aspect of configuration engineering occurs when configuring digital and unit operations controllers. This engineering work reviews the strategies and literally translates the diagrams into filled-out configuration worksheets.

Configuration software engineering may include distributed control highway devices such as multiplexer configuration engineering, programmable controller interface unit configuration engineering, digital controller configuration engineering, unit operation controller configuration engineering, trend unit configuration engineering, and console configuration engineering.

b. *Configuration Software Entry*

Configuration software entry is a keypunch and data entry operation. Information from the worksheets filled out in configuration software engineering is entered into an engineer's console. A magnetic machine-loadable image is produced on either a floppy or hard disk and console-generated printouts.

Following the configuration entry is a visual check comparing the printouts with the worksheets. This check is to correct any errors that may have been introduced during entry.

c. *Special Computer Software Implementation*

Special computer software programs are written, entered into the computer, compiled, debugged, and tested. This testing is limited to a checkout of the software running in the stand-alone computer. Input/output data is manually manipulated to check functionality.

Further analysis of system loading, execution speeds, and memory allocation will be done. The memory usage information should be very accurate. The estimates of system loading and execution speeds will improve but cannot be finalized until the system operates in the final operating environment.

d. *Documentation Services*

i. Drawings

The drawings include symbols denoting special functions of the controllers, such as Scientific Apparatus Manufacturers Association (SAMA) diagrams. The organization and generation of these drawings correlates the configuration software with the process interfacing (loop drawings) of the system.

ii. Loop Drawings

Loop drawings show the wiring connections between the field transducers and the control instrumentation. The drawings are completed with information from the I/O list and the control definition section of the specification.

iii. Operator's Guide

The operator's guide is generated to orient and train the users in the operation of their process through the man–machine interface. It is organized around specific references to the displays, control, and other database information created as a result of configuration engineering.

iv. Engineer's Manual

The engineer's manual serves as a reference for the process or control system engineer. It is the documentation link between the hardware and software and contains information required to understand and modify the control system. It contains information such as the control loop address within controller hardware, the most detailed level of control strategy description, and cross-references to console address.

v. Power and Grounding Drawings

Power and grounding drawings usually consist of three types of drawings for cabinets and consoles: ac power and ground, dc power and ground, and power failure alarm wiring.

vi. Cabinet and Console Layout Drawings

Cabinet and console drawings show the arrangement and dimensions of cabinets and consoles in the control room.

vii. Special Computer Software Manuals

The documentation phase follows the completion of the special computer software implementation work. The user's manual explains the functionality of the system and how the operator interacts with it. The reference manual explains the software structure and technical design for subsequent system modifications and the resolution of technical questions. It consists of the program listings, a detailed operation explanation, flowcharts showing software structure, and database layout diagrams. Also included are variable listings and subprogram names.

e. *Special Staging*

i. Buyout Hardware Integration and Testing

The integration and testing of buyout hardware (that is any nonstandard equipment or any devices not in the supplier price books), includes receiving inspection, physical assembly, system functional testing, and customer acceptance testing.

ii. Configuration Software Integration and Testing

Configuration software integration and testing is a customer acceptance procedure in which the configuration software is downloaded into the system hardware. This activity will verify that the configuration software can be downloaded into the respective devices and that related device configurations (such as consoles and controllers) will function together. The procedure will also give an indication of loading. Final loading will be determined by actual plant conditions.

External I/O connections can be manually or dynamically (through process simulation) applied for testing of configurations, tracing control strategies, and verification of the operator interface. Check-off reports are provided as a record of the testing.

iii. Special Computer Software Integration
    and Testing

The testing and integration of special computer software involves loading the software into the system hardware, functionally checking it, and demonstrating it to the user. This test has the benefit of exercising the software with the completely integrated system hardware and configuration software.

iv. Cabinet Wiring

Cabinet wiring consists of wiring termination panels to controller I/O or wiring connections between controllers. A wiring list is developed to identify the wiring connections necessary, then the actual wiring is completed. Loop drawings detailing this wiring can be provided as a separate service.

v. Panel Assembly and Wiring

Panel assembly and wiring provides the installation and checkout of buyout hardware in a panel or auxiliary console at a staging facility. A wiring list is developed to identify the connections required, the hardware is mounted as appropriate, and the actual wiring is completed. Checkout consists of applying power and verifying operability.

f. *Special Training Implementation*

Special training implementation is simply the execution of the special training as defined in the project specification. Typically, this training is for the operator and uses a combination of configuration software, special computer software, and the operator's guide. The configuration software would include that prepared for the user's application, special controller software for process simulation, and modified console configuration software to enhance the educational content of the school.

The basic on-site school provides a static demonstration of the console displays for familiarization of their content. This process may be enlarged to include the use of special manuals and very rudimentary techniques that make the process appear to be dynamic. It may also involve process simulation (in controllers) to allow the operator to become familiar with and develop expertise for the relationships between loops. This type of training will allow a "tutor" to introduce disturbances and monitor an operator's performance from an external console.

g. *Buyout Procurement*

Buyout procurement is the purchase and order follow-up of the equipment defined in the specification phase. This function includes negotiation of terms and conditions, pricing, establishment of delivery requirements, and tracking of the order from the vendor's manufacturing cycle to arrival at the staging site.

6. START-UP SERVICE

Start-up services consist of any on-site service involved with hardware or software such as process start-up, checkout, acceptance, and tuning. These services are performed by the field service or systems engineering departments.

Start-up services, including travel to the customer's site, are priced on an hourly basis per engineer or technician and include all travel and living expenses.

a. *Installation Supervision Service*

A service engineer monitors and checks the installation of all power grounding equipment and other installation activities for conformity to published specifications. The service engineer provides the user with a weekly list of items checked and documents any items that do not comply with supplier-recommended installation practices.

b. *Hardware Start-Up*

A service engineer should be on-site while the instrumentation is being started up. The engineer's function is to quickly identify malfunctioning equipment and to advise operating personnel of the functional operation of the system.

c. *Panel Checkout*

Panel checkout involves the checkout and hardware startup of the panel equipment. This includes a check of the power and grounding of the panel equipment, a check of all connections to other control system equipment (racks, consoles, computers, motor controls, termination panels, etc.), and the verification of the correct functional operation of each included device.

d. *Instrument Calibration*

A service engineer checks the calibration of the control instrumentation specified in an attachment to the user's purchase order.

All specified equipment is inspected to verify that installation is in accordance with published specifications. Any calibration required to meet published accuracy is included. This does not include start-up or system service.

e. *Configuration Software Start-Up*

Once the hardware is started up and all calibration work is complete, configuration software start-up provides for loading the configuration software into the system and correcting any system errors that result. Depending on the control complexity, this function may have several different levels. The first is simply a start-up with the system under manual control. Next, the system is placed in automatic. If the control strategy employs extensive optimization routines, the process supervision is the next highest loop that is part of the hierarchical control scheme.

During configuration software start-up, it is not unusual for configuration software changes to be made because of error correction and last-minute changes to the process. The person responsible for configuration software start-up must also take responsibility for changing the affected system documentation (drawings and manuals).

f. *Loop Tuning*

Loop tuning is closely related to the activity described in configuration software start-up. Loop tuning, by itself, is the adjustment of the tuning parameters to characterize the selected PID algorithm to the response time of the loop.

g. *Special Computer Software Start-Up*

The start-up of special computer software follows the start-up of the computer hardware equipment. This service provides for loading the software into the computer equipment, initialization work, and methodical start-up and checkout of each software function.

h. *On-Site Acceptance Test*

The on-site acceptance test is the final item prior to formal system acceptance by the customer. This test consists of methodically proceeding through the checklist developed in the earlier section. As each item is successfully demonstrated, it is checked off. Finally, when the checkout is complete, the system is accepted by the user, who then has formal responsibility for it. The date the document is signed corresponds to the system start-up date for system warranty purposes.

5

Steam Plant Management

At present, the areas of steam plant management receiving the most attention are the upgrading of boiler instrumentation for better control, steam generation optimization, optimum steam distribution, and the optimum allocation of fuels. Regardless of the size and complexity of a particular power plant in terms of steam production equipment and distribution system, its objective is the production of steam at the least cost and the satisfaction of the steam users' demand variations.

A. Upgrading Boiler Instrumentation for Better Control

Many industrial boilers installed prior to 1970 are instrumented with minimum control hardware. Because of the low fuel costs at that time, the justification for a sophisticated control strategy and its associated instruments did not exist. In view of today's escalating fuel costs, however, the upgrading of instrumentation for boilers with more than a 40,000-lb/hr rate capacity yields a good ROI. It requires low capital investment and has a good payback (i.e., less than 2 years).

Computer-based energy management systems rely on existing instrumentation to supervise and optimize boiler operation with respect to operating cost.

Table 5.1 shows the improvement that can be made on typical, substandard, existing instrumentation in the three major control systems: combustion, feedwater, and furnace pressure. The upgrading of boiler instrumentation and controls improves efficiency, transient response, and system stability.

Automatic O_2 correction to control excess air in the flue gas can improve boiler efficiency. This automatic control also compensates for varying Btu values of fuels. Such compensation is particularly important for multifuel-firing boilers. The control objectives are the

TABLE 5.1
The Upgrading of Boiler Instrumentation[a]

Control loop	Typical existing situation	Minimum improvement	Desirable improvement
Combustion controls	Parallel positioning type	Change to parallel positioning with steam-flow/air-flow correction	Change to metered control system with cross-limiting and O_2 trim control for operating at maximum efficiency
Feedwater controls	Single-element control system with single-mode control action	Change to two-element control system and two-mode control action	Add three-element control system for best response to load changes
Furnace pressure controls	Single-element control system with single-mode control action	Change to single-element control system with two-mode control action	Add feedforward for large load changes

[a] From Cho (1981).

determination of the boiler's lowest O_2 set point, its operation at that point, compliance with EPA regulations on stack emission, and control of CO levels for optimum boiler efficiency.

Figure 5.1 illustrates the effect of two basic process variables, CO and O_2, on boiler efficiency. The objective of the control strategy is the lowering of excess stack air, thus allowing the boiler to operate in the zone of maximum combustion efficiency. However, the boiler must operate within the constraints on the allowable opacity.

It is important to recognize the sensitivity of these variables with respect to the heat loss in flue gases. The ratio of the gradient of unburned fuel loss to that of excess air loss is about six to one. The O_2 trim control, which is most prevalent in industry today, is a viable way to obtain tight fuel–air ratio control. In some cases a CO analyzer is used as an integral part of the combustion control strategy to minimize the total losses.

The most active projects in recent years have been those directed toward the improvement of combustion efficiency. The first approach to energy management projects involves instrumentation up-

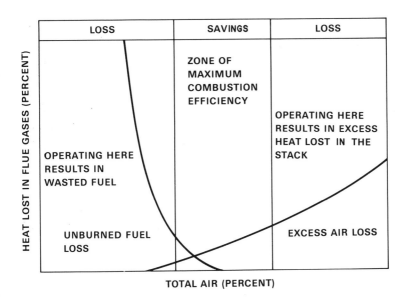

FIG. 5.1 Optimum air for combustion. (From Cho, 1981.)

grading to improve control of for boilers, chillers, cooling towers, etc. Thus individual pieces of equipment can be operated at their level of expected efficiency, thereby reducing energy consumption.

Dedicated microprocessor-based controllers are widely used as an entry-level, low-cost system that can contribute to substantial fuel savings in the powerhouse. These controllers, with single- and multiple-loop capabilities and readily available control, mathematical, and logic functions, can be selected to implement advanced control strategies. Furthermore, these controllers are usually designed to provide an interface to distributed control data highway; they will become a part of the communicating system. The distributed control system can provide a higher-level optimization, which can be carried by the local controllers, allowing the utility complex to be operated from the operator's console.

B. Steam Generation Optimization

Power boilers in industrial plants are controlled to handle demand variations. Typically, the swing boilers are equally loaded and take equal incremental swings that are a function of the variations in the main steam header. This section shows how loads can be allocated among parallel boilers to reduce operating costs.

It is important to recognize under what conditions the optimizer is applicable. When a boiler house has three boilers with a maximum capacity of 300,000 lb/hr, there exists, on the average, a 20–30% reserve capacity for load allocation. When the optimizer is used, energy savings and the resulting cost reductions are expected to be about 1–2% of current energy costs.

Our objective is the least-cost operation of multiple boilers supplying steam to a plant. The optimizer solves the problem of how to allocate the steam load among n boilers, taking the total operating cost as the objective function to be minimized by the allocation (see Fig. 5.2). The objective can be concisely stated by

$$\sum_{i=1}^{n} C_i \quad \text{for} \quad \sum_{i=1}^{n} L_i = D, \tag{5.1}$$

where C_i is dollars per hour for boiler i, L_i pounds per hour for boiler i, and D pounds per hour of load demand.

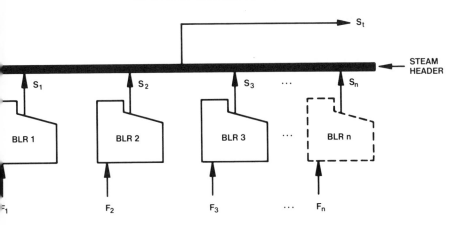

FIG. 5.2   Parallel boilers, where F is the fuel flow, S the steam flow, and S_t the total steam flow. (From Cho, 1978.)

Before we can proceed with a detailed discussion of boiler load allocation we must first understand the energy management calculations for boiler optimization. These are presented in the next section.

1. BOILER PARAMETER CALCULATIONS

Calculations based on field inputs provide important process plant information that will be used for alarming, logging, controlling and optimizing. Typical calculations performed as the prerequisite to boiler load allocation include boiler heat-loss efficiency with single or multiple fuels, boiler I/O efficiency, multiple fuel boiler efficiency when one fuel is not measured, steam properties including enthalpy, entropy, and specific volume, and water properties.

The documentation for the calculation is presented in Table 5.2. The assignable parameters for the calculation include the calculation description, the active–inactive status of the calculation, and the period of execution. To perform the calculation one first enters a constant value for air humidity and stores the value into the database for use during the boiler heat loss (BHL) operation. Next, for the case of coal fired boilers, the inferred coal flow analog input is read from the database and multiplied by 2000 to convert it from tons to pounds. Though these first two procedures are not neces-

TABLE 5.2
Documentation of Boiler Efficiency Calculations[a]

Calculation number	Parameters	Operations
1	A, Constant value	7E − 03
2	ST, Storage location	1 Air humidity
3	LO, Load database index (TTIIII)	10004 BLR 1 coal flow
4	K, Multiplier value	2000
5	ST, Storage location	3 BLR #1 coal flow
6	BHL, User data element for storage	6 BLR 1 efficiency (heat loss)
	Index (GGUU) for fuel analysis	501
	Index (GGUU) for fixed data	201
7	End	

[a] From Blevins *et al.* (1980).

sary, they are included to show the normal mathematical capabilities of the calculation package. Step 6, the BHL operation, calculates boiler heat-loss efficiency. The user-specified operation parameters include the database location for storing the calculated efficiency, the group and unit numbers for fuel analysis data, and the group and unit numbers for the boiler input information. Table 5.3 shows the fuel analysis data and Table 5.4 shows the input information on boiler data. When the calculation shown in Table 5.2 is active, the

TABLE 5.3
Database for Fuel Data Used in Heat-Loss Efficiency Calculations[a]

Element	Description type (number-limited)	Value
1	Carbon (wt %)	72
2	Hydrogen (wt %)	4.4
3	Oxygen (wt %)	3.6
4	Nitrogen (wt %)	1.4
5	Sulfur (wt %)	1.6
6	Water (wt %)	8
7	Ash (wt %)	9
8	Heating value of fuel (Btu/lb)	12,800

[a] From Blevins *et al.* (1980).

TABLE 5.4
Database for Fixed Boiler Data Used in Heat-Loss
Efficiency Calculations[a]

Element	Description type	Value
1	DB (TTIIII) for stack O_2[a]	XXX %
2	DB (TTIIII) for air temp[a]	XXX °F
3	DB (TTIIII) for stack temp[a]	XXX °F
4	DB (TTIIII) for air humidity[a]	XXX %
5	Radient heat loss[b]	3 %
6	Unmeasured heat loss[b]	2 %
7	Combustibles in refuse[b]	10.6 %

[a] Database location TTIII. From Blevins *et al.* (1980).
[b] Values are in percentage and are number-limited.

number one boiler efficiency is periodically calculated using live boiler data.

The cost of operating a boiler can be computed using

$$C_i = K_i L_i / e(L_i), \tag{5.2}$$

where C_i is the dollar-per-hour cost of operating, boiler i, L_i the load on boiler i in million Btu's per hour, K_i the fuel cost in dollars per million Btu's, and $e(L_i)$ the efficiency of the boiler at the given load, L_i, in Btu's per hour. Equation (5.2) shows that the cost of operating a boiler is inversely proportional to its efficiency. The first objective, then, is to improve boiler efficiency as much as possible to ensure the minimum operating cost of individual boilers.

2. BOILER LOAD ALLOCATION

There are two widely known methods of boiler load allocation. They are the individual unit cost technique and the total cost allocation technique. These two methods shall be fully discussed with respect to their individual advantages and disadvantages.

a. *Individual Unit Cost Technique*

The load allocation optimizer is designed to operate the multiple-boiler complex with a number of swing boilers having reserve capacities that can be allocated to minimize the steam production cost. Equation (5.3) shows the relationship between total steam production and boiler operating constraints:

$$\sum_{i=1}^{N} L_i = D \quad \text{and} \quad \text{min} \leq L_i \leq M_i, \tag{5.3}$$

where N is the number of boilers, D the steam demand in thousands of pounds per hour, min the minimum steaming rate of boiler i in thousands of pounds per hour, and M the maximum steaming rate of boiler i in thousands of pounds per hour.

With the use of Lagrangian multipliers, it can be shown that the optimum or least cost for a group of boilers operating in parallel is obtained when the incremental cost for each boiler about the individual unit operating point is equal. This is sometimes known as the principal of equal incremental cost, and it can be shown as

$$\frac{dC(L_1)}{dL_1} = \frac{dC(L_2)}{dL_2} = \frac{dC(L_3)}{dL_3} = \cdots = \frac{dC(L_N)}{dL_N} \quad (\$/1000 \text{ lb}). \tag{5.4}$$

Figure 5.3 is a functional diagram representing the application of the individual unit cost allocation (IUCA) technique to single fuel boilers. For boiler load allocation, the master demand variable is steam header pressure; the master demand controller (MOC) set point is the operator-entered pressure set point; and the feedforward control is the steam flow from the process units. Configuration requirements include minimum and maximum parameters (steam flow and fuel flow, respectively) and status considerations are those of the computer interface equipment, digital control loop, transmitter, boiler feedwater level, boiler draft pressure, and boiler auxiliary equipment.

The allocation objective is the optimal loading of boilers, based on operating economics. Units in selection are determined by the firing demands on each boiler. The digital control regulates set-point coordination and output of firing demand on individual boilers.

The IUCA technique is an improved control method for header pressure and boiler firing demand. It establishes optimum boiler selection to handle steam demand increases and decreases. It also incorporates feedforward compensation for demand changes in major steam users. Decoupling the header-pressure control to the individual boilers results in better header-pressure maintenance.

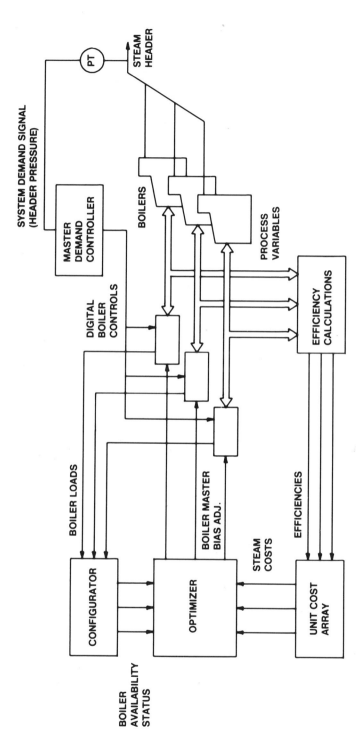

FIG. 5.3   Boiler load allocation using the IUCA technique.

Figure 5.3 shows a configuration in which the local digital controllers are used to implement boiler control systems while a custom computer system generates the optimum load allocation set points for the parallel boilers. This strategy can be readily implemented with a distributed control system.

b. Total Cost Allocation Technique

The total cost allocation (TCA) technique may be implemented in a powerhouse having four swing boilers, such as the one shown in Fig. 5.2.

i. Boiler Characterization

The model used in the boiler characterization is a quadratic efficiency curve determined by a regression analysis performed on pertinent boiler variables. The quadratic curve is

$$e(L) = aL^2 + bL + c, \tag{5.5}$$

where $0 \leq L \leq M$, $e(L)$ is the boiler efficiency in percent as a function of load, a, b, c are the coefficients to be determined by measured data and regression, L is the boiler load in pounds per hour or Btu's per hour, and M is the maximum boiler capacity in pounds per hour.

ii. Boiler Operating Costs

After the efficiency curve for a boiler has been determined, its operating cost can be obtained by the equation

$$C(L) = K_1 L / e(L), \tag{5.6}$$

where $C(L)$ is the boiler operating cost in dollars per hour at L and K_1 is the fuel cost in dollars per 10^6 Btu's.

iii. Total Cost Solution Satisfying the Principle of Equal Incremental Cost

The total cost solution satisfying the principle of equal incremental cost (the slope of the cost curve for some given load) becomes a basis for the optimum boiler load allocation among the number of boilers n supplying the plant. The derivative of Eq. (5.6) with respect to the load is

$$C(L) = \frac{dC(L)}{dL} = \frac{K_2(-aL^2 + c)}{(aL^2 + bL + c)^2},\qquad(5.7)$$

where $C(L)$ is the incremental cost in dollars per 10^6 Btu's of steam and K_2 is the number of dollars per 10^6 Btu's of steam.

iv. Method of Solution (Nelder and Mead, 1967)

The solution technique used is the Nelder–Mead simplex, which is computationally very economical because of the absence of derivatives. This method was originally intended for unconstrained minimization, but in our subprogram it is modified to handle constraints by using a penalty function. The function to be minimized is the sum of the cost curves for each of the n boilers:

$$f(L_1, \ldots, L_n) = \sum_{i=1}^{n} C_i.\qquad(5.8)$$

v. A Four-Boiler Example (Cho, 1978)

Load allocation among parallel boilers is not simple; an operator cannot intuitively arrive at the least-cost solution. Therefore, most industrial boilers take savings in equal increments in response to steam demand. Let us consider an example.

There are four boilers with the following capacities: No. 1 has 120,000 lb/hr, No. 2, 80,000 lb/hr, No. 3, 80,000 lb/hr, and No. 4, 120,000 lb/hr. In Fig. 5.4 we calculated and plotted boiler efficiency based on the plant's steam-generation log sheet. Boiler data were further regressed to obtain a set of four equations representing each boiler:

No. 1,

$$e(L)_1 = -3.618 \times 10^{-10}L_1^2 + 1.733 \times 10^{-5}L_1 + 86;$$

No. 2,

$$e(L)_2 = -3.656 \times 10^{-10}L_2^2 + 9.187 \times 10^{-6}L_2 + 85;$$

No. 3,

$$e(L)_3 = -8.14 \times 10^{-10}L_3^2 + 9.125 \times 10^{-5}L_3 + 85;$$

No. 4,

$$e(L)_4 = -6.0 \times 10^{-10}L_4^2 + 9.5 \times 10^{-5}L_4 + 84.$$

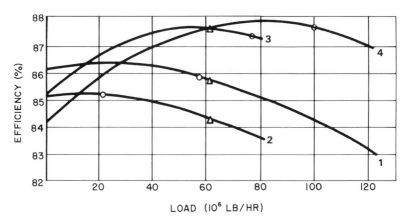

FIG. 5.4 Boiler efficiency versus load showing user-specified (△) and least-cost (○) data points. (From Cho, 1978.)

Fuel costs for each boiler and the above equations become the bases for the generation of the incremental cost for each boiler. The application of the Nelder–Mead method provides optimum load allocation as discussed in the previous section.

Figure 5.5 shows the incremental cost for each boiler. The optimizer program searches for the load that each boiler should carry for a given plant steam demand. The given conditions are a user-specified allocation of 62,500-lb/hr per boiler for a total of 250,000 lb/hr and a fuel cost of $2/10^6 Btu.

The tally for least-cost and user-specified load allocations appears in Table 5.5. Based on data from 350 operating days per year, the potential savings for this example come to $36,000.

vi. Application Modules

There are six basic software modules involves in the implementation of the boiler load optimizer. These are calculation, handler, operator interface, boiler configuration, boiler control, and optimization.

The calculation support module performs data acquisition and calculation, providing engineering information for optimization including on-line boiler efficiency calculation and performance of heat exchangers, if desired.

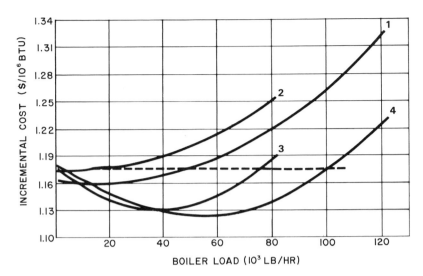

FIG. 5.5   Incremental costs of boilers. (From Cho, 1978.)

The handler module supervises optimization and control by deciding when to optimize, coordinating other modules, monitoring parameters for checks on boiler models and instrument status, and reporting optimization results.

The operator interface optimization program uses many con-

TABLE 5.5
Cost Comparison of Load Allocation Methods[a]

Boiler (lb/hr steam)	Least cost	User specified
1	51,698.1	62,500
2	21,485.7	62,500
3	75,722.2	62,500
4	101,094.0	62,500
Total	250,000.0	250,000
Cost ($/hr)	575.60	579.98
Savings ($/hr for user specified − $/hr for least cost)	4.38 (or $36,000/yr)	

[a] From Cho (1978).

straints to limit the range of such key variables as boiler reserve capacity, fuel cost, electrical cost, and boiler status.

Optimization must answer two important questions: which boilers should be running and what loads should they be assigned? The boiler configuration module indicates which boilers are available for optimization.

The boiler control module functions mainly in a supervisory or direct digital control for actual implementation of boiler load allocation. If advisory control is preferred, this module is not needed.

Optimization software, the heart of this system, determines the load that each boiler shall carry. The solution yields the total and individual operating costs as well as equal loading cost for comparison.

C. Optimum Allocation of Fuels

Optimum fuel allocation of both purchased and by-product fuels is the single most important factor in obtaining substantial reductions in expensive purchased fuel costs (Andreason and Seeman, 1981). The objective of a fuel-management system is the provision of real-time information about by-product and purchased fuels. The system should detail the availability and consumption of both kinds of fuel so that an economic fuel dispatch can be made to maximize the use of by-product fuels, either automatically or by fuel dispatch personnel.

There may be as many as five or six different fuels available for combustion processes. For example, a steel mill may have coke-oven gas, blast-furnace gas, and coal tar as by-product fuels, as well as natural gas and No. 6 oil as purchased fuels. The other industries that have traditionally relied on by-product fuels for large portions of steam generation and cogeneration are the pulp and paper and the chemical industries. For example, in the pulp and paper industry both bark and recovery boilers and power boilers are needed to generate enough steam for the large load demands. The recovery boiler operation is a chemical reduction process unit burning black liquor. The chemical industry may have CO, hydrogen, and process off-gases having combustible elements.

In general, the complexity levels of boiler fuel management can be classified, in order of difficulty, as single-fuel boilers, multifuel boilers, and multifuel boilers with some fuels having variable availability.

The optimization of single-fuel boilers on a common header is the simplest steam optimization problem. Typically, all boilers will utilize the same fuel, thus the major distinguishing factor among the boilers is efficiency.

Fuel availability factors such as curtailment and limit clauses in fuel contracts have caused a decline in the use of single fuels in boilers. Therefore, more boilers are burning different fuels simultaneously. Under these circumstances, boiler efficiency is no longer the major distinguishing factor in fuel utilization optimization. Fuel costs must also be considered. With multifuel boilers, setting the steam load is not enough to optimize steam production. The individual fuel utilization of each boiler must be set instead. This is referred to as boiler fuel optimization.

The sharp rise in the price of purchased fuels such as gas, oil, and coal has forced many companies to install new boilers or to convert existing boilers to burning process off-gases or waste streams along with primary fuels. These waste streams have a low cost, but their varying availability is a major problem. Typically, the boiler operator is responsible for the utilization of these waste fuels in the boilers as they are available; thus at times a waste fuel may be flared instead of being utilized to produce low-cost steam. To optimize fuel utilization in this situation, the boiler steam demand controls must be combined with waste-fuel availability controls to set both the purchased-fuel and waste-fuel usage on the boilers. This is a fuel optimization problem with multiple demand controllers.

1. ALLOCATION OBJECTIVE

Simply stated, the allocation objective for waste-fuel firing is the utilization of the available waste fuel in the appropriate boilers. This utilization results in minimized purchased-fuel usage and, most importantly, lower total steam production costs. When additional waste fuel is available, it should be burned in a boiler in which a purchased fuel is being burned in the most costly manner. Mathematically, the waste-fuel allocation objective can be derived by first looking at the derivation of the general allocation objective for multiple boilers.

Consider multiple boilers all burning gas, oil, and a waste fuel.

The optimization objective is the minimization of the total cost of steam production. Steam production costs can be defined as

$$\$_T = C_g \times F_g^1 + C_o \times F_o^1 + \cdots + C_g \times F_g^n + C_o \times F_o^n, \quad (5.9)$$

where C_g and C_o are the cost of gas and oil, F_g^1 and F_o^1 the utilization of gas and oil on boiler 1, and n the number of boilers.

Note that in Eq. (5.9) waste fuel does not contribute to the cost of steam production because, in this example, it is considered to be free. We wish to minimize the total cost of steam production $\$_T$ with the constraint

$$S_T = S_1 + S_2 + \cdots + S_n, \quad (5.10)$$

where S_T is the total steam production, which is the sum of the individual boiler steam loads.

The Lagrange multiplier technique can be used to analyze this optimization problem. This technique shows that a necessary condition for $\$_T$ to achieve a maximum or minimum is

$$\partial H/\partial S_i = 0, \quad i = 1, n, \quad (5.11)$$

where H is defined as

$$H = \$_T + \lambda S_T. \quad (5.12)$$

The constant λ is the Lagrangian multiplier. Combining Eqs. (5.11) and (5.12) gives

$$\frac{\partial H}{\partial S_i} = \frac{\partial S_T}{\partial S_i} + \lambda \frac{\partial S_T}{\partial S_i} = 0, \quad i = 1, n. \quad (5.13)$$

Equation (5.13) can be simplified by using Eq. (5.10) to eliminate the derivative $\partial S_T/\partial S_i$, since this derivative will equal one for all boilers. The resulting set of n equations is

$$\frac{\partial \$_T}{\partial S_1} + \lambda = 0,$$

$$\frac{\partial \$_T}{\partial S_2} + \lambda = 0,$$

$$\vdots$$

$$\frac{\partial \$_T}{\partial S_n} + \lambda = 0. \quad (5.14)$$

For these n equations to all equal 0, the derivatives must all be equal, or

$$\frac{\partial \$_T}{\partial S_1} = \frac{\partial \$_T}{\partial S_2} = \cdots = \frac{\partial \$_T}{\partial S_n} = -\lambda. \tag{5.15}$$

If Eq. (5.9) is rewritten as

$$\$_T = \$_1 + \$_2 + \cdots + \$_n, \tag{5.16}$$

then Eq. (5.15) can be rewritten as

$$\frac{\partial \$_1}{\partial S_1} = \frac{\partial \$_2}{\partial S_2} = \cdots = \frac{\partial \$_n}{\partial S_n} = -\lambda. \tag{5.17}$$

This is a general expression of the allocation objective for optimization. To minimize steam cost, the individual boiler steam production costs represented in Eq. (5.17) must be equal. However, since each boiler is burning three fuels, there are three cost terms per boiler that must be used. For Boiler 1 the cost terms are

$$\frac{\partial \$_1}{\partial S_1}\bigg|_{F_o^1, F_w^1} \qquad \text{for} \quad \text{gas as swing fuel,} \tag{5.18}$$

$$\frac{\partial \$_1}{\partial S_1}\bigg|_{F_g^1, F_w^1} \qquad \text{for} \quad \text{oil as swing fuel,} \tag{5.19}$$

$$\frac{\partial \$_1}{\partial S_1}\bigg|_{F_g^1, F_o^1} \qquad \text{for} \quad \text{waste fuel as swing fuel,} \tag{5.20}$$

where F_w^1 is the waste-fuel utilization on the first boiler.

For header steam demand changes, one must choose between gas and oil firing on the boilers to meet steam demand. Mathematically, the allocation objective for the steam demand control would be expressed, using the cost terms from Eqs. (5.18)–(5.20), as

$$\frac{\partial \$_1}{\partial S_1}\bigg|_{F_o^1, F_w^1} = \frac{\partial \$_1}{\partial S_1}\bigg|_{F_g^1, F_w^1} = -\lambda. \tag{5.21}$$

The same would be true for other boilers; all boilers must have equal gas and oil steam production cost terms.

Waste-fuel utilization must be set by a header-pressure demand controller that is independent of the steam demand controller. When a change occurs in waste-fuel utilization, steam production should theoretically remain constant. This is accomplished by changing purchased-fuel firing as a result of a waste-fuel change, based on an equal steam production exchange. Therefore, a waste-fuel allocation objective that would be equivalent to the one expressed in Eqs. (5.18)–(5.20) must calculate the steam cost based on exchanging two fuels at constant steam load. This objective can be represented mathematically, first for gas exchanged with waste fuel and then for oil exchanged with waste fuel on Boiler 1 as follows:

$$\text{gas:} \quad \left.\frac{\partial \$_1}{\partial S_1}\right|_{S_1, F_o^l} = \left.\frac{\partial \$_1}{\partial S_1}\right|_{F_w^l, F_o^l} - \left.\frac{\partial \$_1}{\partial S_1}\right|_{F_g^l, F_o^l}; \qquad (5.22)$$

$$\text{oil:} \quad \left.\frac{\partial \$_1}{\partial S_1}\right|_{S_1, F_g^l} = \left.\frac{\partial \$_1}{\partial S_1}\right|_{F_w^l, F_g^l} - \left.\frac{\partial \$_1}{\partial S_1}\right|_{F_o^l, F_g^l} \qquad (5.23)$$

Similar objectives can be defined for the other boilers. These equations show the change in steam production costs resulting from the exchange of waste fuel for purchased fuel. The allocator technique allows one to look at the costs on each boiler and determine where waste fuel should be increased or decreased as availability changes. If more waste fuel becomes available, the waste-fuel allocator would choose the boiler and purchased fuel that are producing steam at the highest cost. Using a control scheme, the waste fuel would then be increased and the purchased fuel decreased to maintain constant steam production. To calculate the fuel exchange, this control takes into account fuel heating values and boiler efficiency. The allocator must also ascertain the ability of a boiler to burn waste fuel, based on the steam production constants and purchased-fuel utilization limits.

The solution to the waste-fuel allocation problem requires two demand controllers operating in parallel. The steam demand controller sets the level of purchased fuel usage and the waste-fuel controller sets the level of waste-fuel and purchased-fuel usage. The allocation objectives are expressed by Eqs. (5.21)–(5.23) respectively.

In the next section the functional implementation of the allocator will be presented and discussed. The heart of the allocation technique is the unit selector (US) function used in the control implementation. The function of the US will also be discussed.

2. THE CONTROL SCHEME

As an example, we shall discuss two boilers on a common header. Each boiler is fired with two primary fuels, gas and oil, and one waste fuel. Figure 5.6 depicts this arrangement.

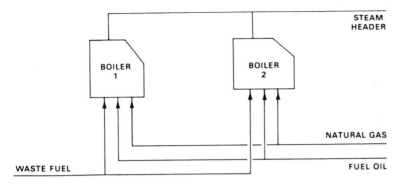

FIG. 5.6   System diagram. (From Andreason and Seemann, 1981.)

The waste fuel could be either a contracted fuel used primarily by a plant process unit or an off-gas from a process unit. If the waste fuel is contracted, that portion of the contract amount not used for process needs is available to be burned in the boilers. If not burned in the boiler, it must be flared, because the contract requires its utilization by the plant. The control objective is the maintenance of the contract usage of the fuel by allocation to the boilers when available and the reduction of the firing of gas and oil.

For the case in which the waste fuel is an off-gas from a process, the control objective is the burning of all waste fuel available. Typically, this would be achieved by maintaining a constant pressure in the waste-fuel header. In our example a waste-fuel header-pressure controller will be used.

Figure 5.7 is a functional representation of a scheme to control steam header pressure and waste header pressure by manipulating gas, oil, and the waste-fuel utilization on the two boilers. In Fig. 5.7 only the individual fuel and air controls for one boiler are represented.

The steam demand is met by the allocation of primary fuels. The waste-fuel header pressure is controlled by allocation of the waste fuel and one primary fuel.

The steam header-pressure control consists of a pressure controller and a US, which replace the standard boiler master. These functions constitute the intelligent plant and boiler masters. The incremental output of the pressure controller is passed to the intelligent

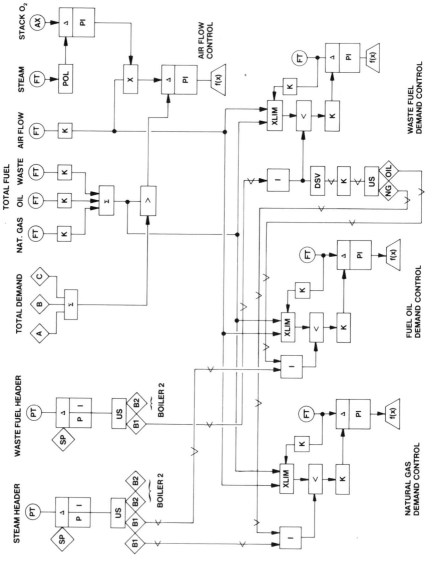

FIG. 5.7 Functional representation of a control scheme, where ∨ is an incremental signal. (From Andreyev and Siemens, 1981.)

US. The US then examines the cost data for each fuel on each boiler and allocates the required demand change to the most economical fuel, taking into account process constraints and abnormal conditions that prevent allocation.

For this example, the individual fuel controls are in the computer; they manage the adjustment of the individual fuel demands to meet steam requirements. The natural gas demand control loop will control the flow of natural gas to the limit allowed by air. In this fuel demand control, the multiple input limit block examines total fuel usage, total air, and current natural gas usage to determine the allowable natural gas flow for the current combustion air limits. The low selector will pass the current natural gas demand or the allowable natural gas flow to the set point at the natural gas controller.

The fuel-oil-demand control works in the same manner as the natural gas-demand control, allowing individual fuel–air cross limits on each fuel and, more importantly, between fuels. Cross limits are important when waste fuel is being exchanged with a primary fuel. These limits will allow an increase in waste-fuel firing to occur only as the primary fuel is decreased. This prevents the boiler from becoming fuel-rich.

The operation of the waste-fuel demand control is similar to that of the natural-gas-demand control but has the added ability to trade changes in waste-fuel demand with corresponding changes in primary fuel demand. Changes in waste-fuel demand are detected by the deviation select value (DSV) function and passed to another US function. The US function then decides whether oil or gas is the most cost-effective fuel to trade with waste fuel.

The fuel-demand calculator sums the demands for each fuel. This total is used in the air cross limit to determine the air-control set point.

The fuel calculator sums the current fuel flows to calculate total fuel Btu's. This total fuel signal is used to determine the combustion air-control set point. The signal is also used in the individual fuel-flow demand controls.

The combustion air is either the total demand or the total fuel, whichever is greater. This is analogous to a single-fuel combustion-air set point being the greater of the firing rate demand and the total fuel.

An O_2 trim control adjusts the air/fuel ratio to achieve the desired O_2 level for current steam production. Load programming of O_2 with steam is achieved through the polynomial (POL) function, the coefficients of which are determined from boiler load tests.

The technique of allocation through control using an intelligent plant master and unit master is referred to as the IUCA technique. Economic information and unit status information are combined in the US to make an intelligent choice as to the best way to handle demand changes.

3. IMPLEMENTATION OF THE IUCA TECHNIQUE (Blevins *et al.*, 1980)

The IUCA technique is an intelligent control technique. It consists of five major parts, represented in Fig. 5.8. These parts are demand control, unit selection, status calculations and configuration, cost calculations and organization, digital control, and feedforward calculation. Figure 5.8 shows how these individual pieces are linked together to control steam demand in an optimal way.

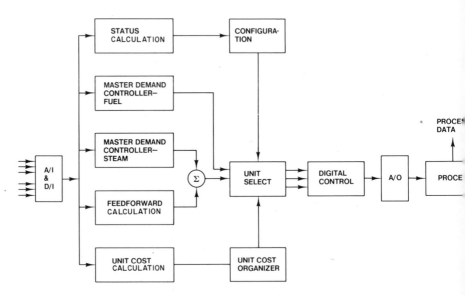

FIG. 5.8   Individual unit cost allocation technique for by-product fuel management. (From Blevins *et al.*, 1980.)

The actual control strategy used will depend on its intended application. To efficiently handle the various applications, it was necessary to develop standardized software functions that could be customized through database specification.

Four software tasks were designed to allow implementation of the IUCA technique. These four tasks are indicated in Fig. 5.8. Two tasks are incorporated as functions in the continuous control application package (CCAP) and two as operations in the energy management calculations package (EMCP). The tasks are the following:

Task	Name
US function	Unit selector
MDC function	Master demand controller
CNF operation	Configuration
UCO operation	Unit cost organizer

The MDC function is a velocity proportional integral derivative (PID) control algorithm. It is used to determine incremental load changes based on the deviation of the demand variable from the set point and the controller tuning constants. This PID algorithm has individual tuning constants per allocation unit; for this example, an allocation unit is a fuel. The incremental load change from the demand controller is passed to the US function which determines, based on cost and configuration data, which unit (or units) should have its (their) loads changed to satisfy the incremental load change request. The US then distributes the load changes to the appropriate units, taking into account individual unit process limits.

The MDC and US functions reside in the same continuous control loop. The individual unit controls may reside in the computer or may be performed by analog devices external to the computer. For this example, all unit controls are in the computer to allow individual fuel manipulation and fuel–air and fuel–fuel cross-limiting.

The configuration portion of the IUCA technique consists of status calculations and the combination of the results of status calculations into two resultant status indications to be used by the US. The status calculations monitor conditions that prevent a unit, such as a boiler, from accepting demand changes from the US. Such conditions are computer interface equipment status, analog controller status, computer input failures, computer control loop status, process variable values compared with limits, and mechanical equipment status.

The CNF operation combines the results of all status calculations per individual allocation unit. The results of status calculations performed through the logic operations available in the EMCP are inputs to the CNF operation. The outputs from the CNF operation are two status indicators—one that permits unit load increases and one that permits unit load decreases. If neither status is in the permissive state, a unit's load cannot be adjusted by the US function.

Cost calculations, performed by the user through the mathematical operations available in the EMCP, determine the unit costs of utility production for each unit in the allocation. For boilers the unit cost objective is the cost per 1000 lb steam. For the US to use this cost information it must be organized in monotonic (continuously increasing) order, which is done by the UCO operation. The UCO operation is an interface task between the calculations that determine unit costs and the final presentation of the cost information to the US.

The final portion of the allocation implementation is the digital control. This, as mentioned earlier, is customized for individual application.

The example being considered has two demand controllers (see Fig. 5.7), one for header pressure and one for waste fuel. The details of the implementation for the steam header-pressure control are as follows.

For steam header-pressure control the master demand variable is steam header pressure; the MDC set point is the operator entered pressure set point. Configuration requirements for the primary fuel on each boiler are its minimum and maximum parameters and status considerations. The minimum and maximum parameters are steam flow and fuel flow, respectively. Status considerations are computer interface equipment status, digital control loop status, transmitter status, boiler feedwater level, and furnace pressure.

The allocation objective for header-pressure control is the optimal loading of boilers. This may be achieved by studying primary-fuel operating economics [see Eq. (5.21)]. Units in selection are determined by the fuel demand for gas and oil on each boiler. Digital control regulates gas and oil flow control, combustion air flow control, tracking controls for analog backup controls, header-pressure controller tracking, and O_2 trim control. Computer outputs include computer–auto–manual station for gas, oil, and combustion air, computer–manual station for header master-output tracking, computer–manual station for boiler master-bias and backup-analog tracking. Analog control determines the analog backup of combustion control and the header-pressure controller.

The details of the implementation for the waste-fuel control are as follows. The master demand variable is the waste-fuel header flow if we are considering contracted fuel and waste-fuel header pressure if we are considering the process unit output; the set point is the operator-entered or contracted fuel flow or operator-entered pressure set point. Configuration requirements for the waste fuel on each boiler are the minimum and maximum parameters, which are steam flow and waste fuel flow, respectively, and status considerations, which are computer interface equipment status, analog waste-fuel controller status, availability of primary fuels, digital control loop status of primary fuel controls, transmitter status, boiler feedwater level, and furnace pressure.

The waste-fuel control allocation objective is the allocation of waste fuel to boilers that obtain the most economical trade-off of primary fuel [See Eq. (5.21)]. Units in selection are determined by the waste-fuel demand for each boiler. Digital control regulates waste-fuel flow control and associated cross-limiting with air and total fuel. Analog backup control determines waste-fuel header flow or pressure indication.

The IUCA technique is an improved method of steam header-pressure and waste-fuel management control. It establishes optimum selection of boilers to handle plant steam demand changes. Most importantly, it allows for the automatic and optimum usage of cheaper waste fuels. The result is minimum steam production costs. If one decouples the steam header-pressure and waste header controls to the individual boilers, better header-pressure maintenance will result.

If one cross-limits individual fuels, the result is fuel cross-limiting based on available air, thus achieving better fuel management on multifuel boilers burning waste fuels with variable availability. This allows better maintenance of stack dry-gas losses, also reducing steam costs.

Although the implementation of a fuel allocation strategy is developed for a centralized computer system with analog backup, the functions defined in this technique can be easily distributed among the devices in a distributed control system if it is warranted.

6

Electrical Power Management

Electrical power is one of the most important energy sources in any plant. The cost of providing the electrical energy necessary for production activities usually constitutes a significant part of the total plant energy costs. For the purpose of developing the concepts and procedures for electrical power management, the topic of plant energy acquisition is subdivided into three major areas: those plants that purchase 100% of their electrical power from a local utility company; those that are totally self-sufficient (i.e., generate all of their electrical power needs); and those that purchase a percentage of the total electrical needs, with the balance being met by in-plant generation.

The specific areas of interest for energy management include the source of a plant's electrical power supply and that plant's operating constraints. When deciding whether to make or buy power, a careful analysis should be made of the potential purchase contract and the plant's operating flexibility. The cost of in-plant generation (including variable steam costs) should be considered, as well as the cost of alternative modes of generation such as back pressure, extraction, and/or condensing.

The four major areas of computer applications for electrical power management are power-demand control, turbogenerator-network management, tie-line control, and cooling tower management. In this chapter the effect of each of these areas on the implementation of an energy management system will be fully explained.

A. Power-Demand Control

In this section, the concepts and philosophy of power-demand control focus plants that are completely dependent on a local utility company for the purchase of their electrical power.

Electrical energy usage is high in most process and manufacturing plants and accounts for a significant portion of overall operating expenses. The two major electrical costs to industrial consumers are based on the total amount of energy used and on the peak demand (the rate at which power is consumed). The energy-use charge is comprised of the operating and fuel costs associated with generation and distribution of electricity. The demand charge is based on the utility company's capital investment in equipment needed to satisfy customer needs.

Depending on the complexity and magnitude of the power-demand control and the number of electrical loads that are to be managed, the power-demand control system can range from a simple and low-cost programmable logic controller to a medium or large computer system. The technology currently available in peak-load control systems can be reasonably well suited for either small or large industrial plants.

1. IDENTIFYING POTENTIALS
(Cho and Dray, 1982)

One of the most effective ways to evaluate and identify a plant's energy-savings potential is to compile a list of the electrical cost components that make up the plant's total electrical energy cost. The list may include the demand charge, energy charge, power-factor charge, load-factor charge, and fuel cost adjustment. These items can serve as a checklist for the electrical cost components that characterize a plant.

To analyze these data it is important to understand the historical trends of the cost components over a year or two. Once a benchmark has been established for each of the categories, the potential cost-savings strategy can be formulated. The first four elements are particularly important because they represent variable costs offering varying degrees of cost-reduction opportunity. Power- and load-factor charges should be evaluated so that the penalties associated with these charges can be minimized.

In general, if a plant's demand charge is greater than 40–50% of the total energy bill, it may be possible to reduce the demand charge by power-demand control.

a. Understanding Demand Charge

Demand is the average power load used by the plant during predetermined intervals—usually 15, 30, or 60 min. Peak demand is the highest kilowatt load obtained during the demand interval within the billing period.

For a demand interval of 1 hr, the plant demand may look something like the graph in Fig. 6.1 (which depicts plant demand from 8:00 a.m. to 4:00 p.m. day shift). The peak demand for this shift is registered in the demand interval between 2:00 and 3:00 p.m. The demand portion of your monthly bill will be based on this peak kilowatt load if it is the peak demand for the month.

b. Procedure for Load-Control Evaluation

Before we can develop a control strategy and implementation plan, we need to know the plant's power-demand characteristics. A histogram such as the one shown in Fig. 6.2, going back, say, 6–12 months, should reveal the plant's peak load-demand patterns and whether they are cyclic or random.

Because the plant load can be minimally classified into base loads and controllable loads, we need to examine and evaluate the controllable loads to investigate the feasibility of redistributing the control-

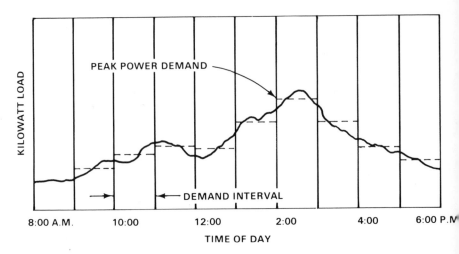

FIG. 6.1   Peak-load demand.

lable loads and/or load-shed program, thereby reducing peak demand.

A detailed study of the plant's controllable loads should contain the name and load in kilowatts, acceptable shed time, shed duration including a minimum and maximum interval, shed potential, and load-shed priorities. Table 6.1 illustrates this format and provides some idea of the possible electrical devices that may be present in the plant.

When selecting load-shed programs for the plant, one must ensure that they do not interrupt production or alter product specification and that they do not create safety hazards or employee discomfort.

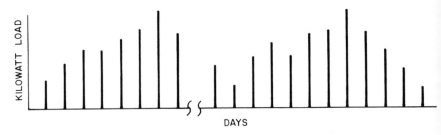

FIG. 6.2   Plant kilowatt demand histogram.

TABLE 6.1
Simple Survey of Controllable Loads

Equipment name	Load (kW)	Shed time	Shed interval (min)	Shed potential	Priority
Fan No. 1	400	8:00–10:00	5	33.3	1
Heater	1500	10:00–13:00	15	375	1
Pumps	60	9:00–11:00	30	30	2
Chillers	—	—	—	—	—
Hot water heater	—	—	—	—	—
Battery chargers	—	—	—	—	—
Furnace	—	—	—	—	—
Dow vaporizer	—	—	—	—	—
Heating and ventilation motors	—	—	—	—	—

2. CONTROL STRATEGY

a. *Leveling Peaks by Load Scheduling*

If possible try to identify the recurring controllable loads that are responsible for setting the peak power demand. In the study period shown in Fig. 6.2, the production schedule and electrical-power-related tasks should be investigated to formulate a strategy allowing redistribution of loads. The main consideration concerning the implementation of this strategy is its effect on production.

This strategy will result in the reduction of the demand portion of your electrical billing, however, there may be no change in the energy consumption (kilowatt hour) charge.

b. *Power-Demand Characteristics*

In most plants precise interval-to-interval power-demand prediction is very difficult, if not impossible, because the plant's load demand is dictated by many uncontrollable conditions and events associated with production. Therefore, power demand should be controlled so that its maximum value corresponds to the predetermined target value. The type of controllable loads shown in Table 6.1, with identified load constraints for each of the loads, becomes a

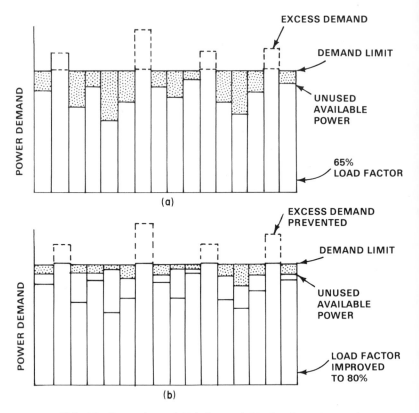

FIG. 6.3   Power demand (a) before and (b) after demand control.

resource from which a load-shed–restore program can be developed and implemented.

Figure 6.3b shows more efficient utilization of contracted electric power as compared to that of Fig. 6.3a. Proper implementation of power-demand control can help prevent excess demand and improve load factors.

3. CONTROL SYSTEMS

Many types of demand-control systems exist on the market today. These range from relatively simple demand controllers to large-scale computer-based systems.

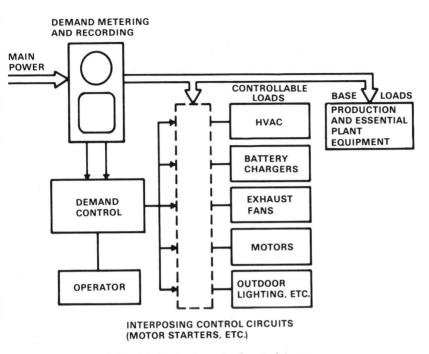

FIG. 6.4   Basic elements of control system.

Intermediate systems offering some flexibility in demand-control programs incorporate programmable logic controllers (PLC) or microprocessor-based control systems. They all perform essentially the same function. The system measures the energy being consumed in a plant and limits demand by turning off nonessential loads or by unloading the controllable loads during the demand-control interval. The basic elements of a control system are shown in Fig. 6.4.

Software should log, display, and control the plant's maximum allowable kilowatt load.

a. Data Acquisition

The energy management system should log, calculate, and display the kilowatt demand for each contracted interval, power factor, and load factor. The total kilowatts per hour for the shift, day, and month should also be calculated as should any other useful information identified by the plant personnel. The inputs of the data acquisition function include kilowatts, kVAR, and demand-interval time (clock).

b. *Power-Demand Control Techniques*

There are at least three well-known techniques for power-demand control: ideal-rate control, instantaneous demand control, and predictive or forecasting control. The selection of one of these methods coupled with a load-shed–restore program dictates the type of control system you will select for your plant.

i. Ideal Rate Control

Ideal rate control can correct errors during the first part of the interval as well as toward its end. For each demand interval an ideal rate (or ramp) of energy usage is used as a set point. This ramp starts at zero and ends at a level of energy consumption that will meet the target demand for the interval. At each control calculation the rate of actual energy usage is compared with this ideal rate, and loads are shed or restored accordingly, as shown in Fig. 6.5.

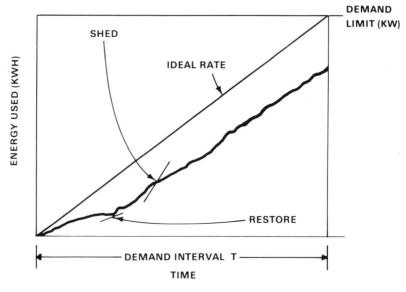

FIG. 6.5   Ideal rate.

Several variations of this control method exist, often under different names. One of these, offset rate control, allows an initial usage greater than zero, thus postponing control actions until later in the interval.

ii. Instantaneous Control

The simplest and most straightforward control scheme is known as instantaneous demand control. This control is comparable to any simple, continuous-process controller. When the instantaneous demand exceeds the target, the controller sheds a load; when the demand falls more than a certain amount below that target demand, a load is restored.

This method will work best in an area where the power company bases its charges on instantaneous demand. In regions where the power company bases its demand charge on average demand over a fixed interval (or accumulated usage over that interval), this control method will not work well (see Fig. 6.6).

iii. Predicted Demand Control

Predicted demand control is an advanced method for controlling electrical power demand. This method ascertains the amount of

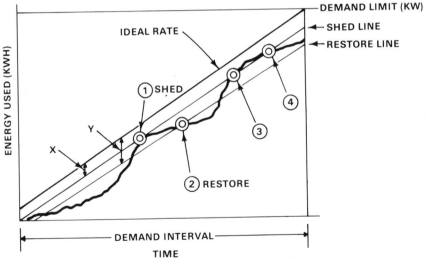

FIG. 6.6   Instantaneous rate.

power used in the first part of an interval, then extrapolates to determine the power required for the remainder of the interval and regulates demand so that average power use over the interval does not exceed the target kilowatt figure. This desired demand is then compared with the present instantaneous demand, and loads are shed or restored to maintain the present demand below that desired. This method of calculation can be depicted as

predicted rate

$$= \frac{\text{kW·h used} - \text{kW·h used at last control point}}{\text{time between control points}}, \quad (6.1)$$

$$\text{max. rate} = \frac{\text{kW·h max.} - \text{kW·h used}}{\text{time interval} - \text{time used}}. \quad (6.2)$$

The predicted and maximum rates can be calculated with Eqs. (6.1) and (6.2). Loads can then be shed or restored to eliminate any difference between these rates. Time between control points is selectable so that control sensitivity can be balanced against frequency of load shedding and restoring (see Fig. 6.7). Also, a software filter

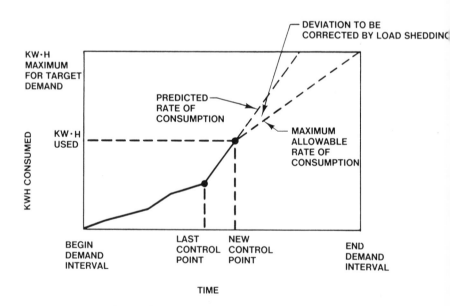

FIG. 6.7   Predicted rate. (From Cho, 1981.)

can be used to reduce the effect of sudden surges in kilowatt-hour consumption.

c. Load Shedding or Restoration

The power-demand control system may use a number of different methods to determine which loads should be restored or shed.

A "ring" is used in a system in which all the loads have approximately the same priority. To shed loads, this system chooses the load that has been on the longest; to restore loads, this system chooses the load that has been shed the longest. The controller moves continuously around the ring, shedding and restoring loads in a continuous sequence. In a ring organization, the first load to be shed is also the first to be restored.

The "priority stack" organizes all loads in a single list with the less important loads (those most easily shed) at the bottom of the list. To shed loads the controller starts at the bottom of the list and works upward; to restore loads the controller starts at the top of the list and works downward, thus restoring the last load that was shed. In a priority stack, the first load to be shed is the last load to be restored.

To provide the greatest adaptability in organizing the shed/restore sequence for any combination of loads, a "dual hierarchy" method was developed to allow the use of any combination of the two sequences described above. A dual hierarchy also provides the capability for individual adjustment of allowable duty cycles and shedding frequencies (see Fig. 6.8).

4. POTENTIAL SAVINGS

The potential savings that can be realized from the implementation of a power-demand control system can be evaluated from recent electric bills and rate schedules. The load-shed potentials of a plant can be determined with the use of a simple equation. The load-shed potential for each load is calculated by

$$\text{load shed potential (kW)} = \frac{\text{kW} \times \text{shed time}}{\text{demand interval}} \cdot \tag{6.3}$$

By subtracting the total load-shed potential from the peak power demand on the plant's electrical bill, it is possible to evaluate the

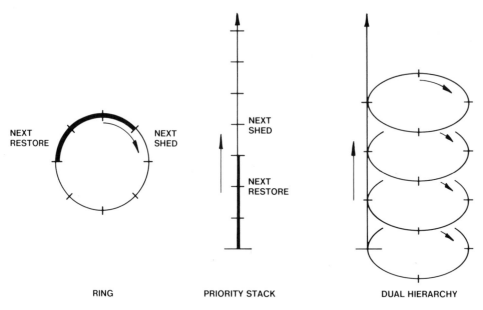

FIG. 6.8   Load-shed–restore organizations. (From Cho, 1981.)

potential cost reduction in the plant's demand charge. For example, a typical rate schedule on demand charge may appear as $2.50/kW for the first 100 kW, $2.00/kW for the next 1000 kW, $1.50/kW for the next 10,000 kW, and $1.25/kW for the next 20,000 kW.

For a selected totaling period let us assume that the demand charge was $39,250.00, based on the plant's peak demand of 29,100 kW. This was computed by the application of the above rate structure. If the load-demand control system is implemented with the load-shed resources shown in Table 6.1, the demand cost saving can be estimated at $6250.00/month.

Small industrial plants can reduce their energy charges by reevaluating their plant load characteristics for leveling demands, taking into consideration production tasks and implementing demand-limiting control systems.

Because of the wide range of control hardware on today's market, it is possible to find the system that is best suited for your plant and that satisfies the cost and payback guidelines for your project.

The basic demand controllers or programmable logic controllers (or microprocessor-based systems) may be quite adequate for a small plant with a simple ideal-control technique. Typically, the system hardware costs range from $20,000 to $60,000. However, project cost estimates should include the installation of equipment and control panel and load control relays (either automatic or manual) as well as basic hardware.

Based on the 10–20% savings on electrical bills reported by various industries and businesses, a payback period of 6 to 12 months may be expected. If other plant utilities can be better managed and controlled, the computer-based power-demand control system may be justified in expanding its capability to control other utility functions such as chilling, steam generation and distribution, and compressed-air system management.

B. Turbogenerator Network Management and Tie-Line Control

Cogeneration is an efficient way to meet electrical and steam demands in process plants. For example, the pulp and paper industry, with its large steam requirements, has used cogeneration for years to supply a portion of its mills' electrical demands. Some mills are even self-sufficient in terms of their electrical power needs. The mills either purchase the balance of their electrical power or contract to purchase electrical energy from a local utility company (via a tie-line) as needed.

Turbogenerator network management focuses on a number of energy-saving opportunities in the process industry. The problems of optimizing steam and power generation can be seen by analyzing the steam balance diagram shown in Fig. 6.9.

The sources of lower-pressure steam dictate their costs. In our example, a 150-psig steam header can be supplied with the steam from a pressure reducing station (PRS), extractions from turbogenerator no. 1 or 2, or any combination thereof. For example, expanding high-pressure steam through a reducing valve and then desuperheating it to saturation temperature can be more costly than expanding the steam through a turbine where the difference in entropy is used to generate power. The same analysis can be applied to a 50-psig steam header with respect to the steam cost because the steam cost has three possible sources, each having a different cost.

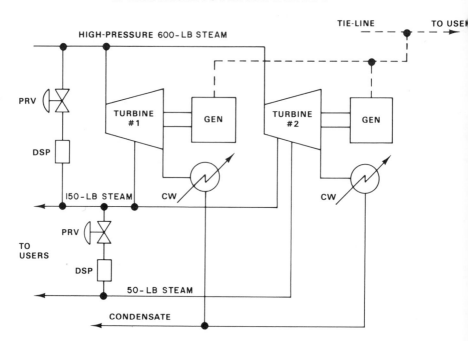

FIG. 6.9 Turbogenerator network. DSP, desuperheating. (From Blevins *et al.*, 1980.)

1. ELECTRICAL POWER MANAGEMENT PHILOSOPHY

The objective of the turbogenerator network management system is the provision of a plant's electrical power at a minimum cost and under the system's operating constraints. The operating factors that have an impact on costs are the decision to make or buy, the optimum allocation of load, the opportunity to sell, and the possibility of self-sufficiency.

a. *Make or Buy Decisions*

The decision to make or buy power should be made with an understanding of the contracted kilowatt demand limit, the time-of-day rates if applicable, the status of steam balance in the distribution headers, and the power-demand control strategy.

b. *Optimum Allocation of Load*

The kilowatt load should be allocated to turbogenerators based on the incremental costs (dollars per kilowatt hour) of each on-line unit. When developing a plant-wide kilowatt load allocation strategy, one should consider the individual steam-pass efficiency associated with turbogenerator extractions as well as condensing generations. This will ensure that low-pressure header balance is maintained by the use of the most economical steam source for load increases and the most expensive sources for load decreases.

c. *Evaluate Opportunity to Sell*

An additional dimension of operating flexibility in achieving optimum in-plant power generation is provided if the local utility company is willing to purchase electrical power from an industrial plant. Because of the higher interdependent nature of steam and electrical power, it is important to develop an operating philosophy and implementation plan that considers the best trade-offs and alternatives and strives toward a least-cost solution to meet the demand for these two utilities.

d. *Self-Sufficient Plants*

Many pulp and paper mills and other industrial plants are self-sufficient in terms of their electrical power. In the self-sufficient plant, which does not have the flexibility of the "make or buy" decision, the economics of cogeneration depends largely on the plant's success in generating electrical power in the condensing mode. Therefore, the load allocation between the condensing generations, taking into consideration the heat rates, is very important.

2. TURBOGENERATOR PERFORMANCE CALCULATIONS

Calculations of turbogenerator performance must be performed before an optimization program can be executed. The turbogenerator calculations may include heat rate, ideal rate, combined steam-path efficiency, and section efficiency.

The heat rate is the number of Btu's used per kilowatt-hour of electrical generation; it is shown as

$$\text{heat rate} = \frac{\sum_{i=1}^{N} F_i(H_i - H_{i+1})}{\text{kW}} \quad \frac{\text{Btu}}{\text{kW·h}}. \qquad (6.4)$$

By comparing the actual heat rate to the ideal heat rate [Btu's available per kilowatt-hour for ideal conditions (isentropic expansion)], a measure of performance is found. The ideal heat rate is given as

$$\text{ideal heat rate} = \frac{\sum_{i=1}^{N} F_i(H_i - IH_{i+1})}{\text{kW}} \quad \frac{\text{Btu}}{\text{kW·h}}, \qquad (6.5)$$

and the combined steam-path efficiency is a ratio of the actual heat rate to the ideal heat rate, which is shown as

$$\text{combined steam-path efficiency} = \frac{\text{heat rate} \times 100}{\text{ideal heat rate}} \% . \quad (6.6)$$

Section efficiency may be calculated as the ratio of actual enthalpy change through the section to that for isentropic expansion, as shown by

$$\text{steam-path efficiency at stage } i = \frac{(H_i - H_{i+1}) \times 100}{(H_i - IH_{i+1})} \% . \quad (6.7)$$

Losses because of mechanical friction, heat radiation, etc., are reflected in the mechanical efficiency, which is the ratio of the Btu equivalent of 1 kW·h, 3412.7 Btu, to the actual Btu's used per kilowatt hour generated. It is given as

$$\text{mechanical efficiency} = \frac{3412.7 \times 100}{\text{heat rate}} \% . \qquad (6.8)$$

Overall turbine efficiency is the product of combined steam-path efficiency and mechanical efficiency, which is shown by

overall efficiency

$$= \frac{(\text{mechanical efficiency})(\text{combined steam-path efficiency})}{100} \% ,$$

$$(6.9)$$

where F_i is the flow through stage i in Btu's per pound, H_i the enthalpy entering stage i in Btu's per pound, H_{i+1} the enthalpy exit-

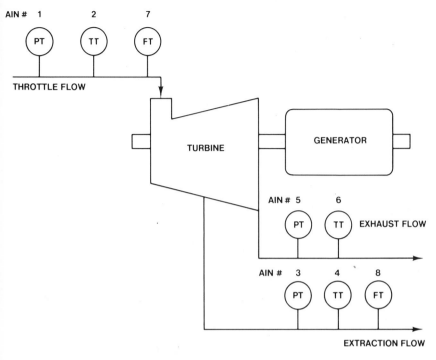

FIG. 6.10 Turbogenerator diagram. PT, pressure transmitter; TT, temperature transmitter; FT, flow temperature; AIN, analog input signal. (From Blevins *et al.*, 1980.)

ing stage i in Btu's per pound, IH_{i+1} the enthalpy existing at stage i if steam expansion were isentropic in Btu's per pound, kW the generator output of kilowatts, and N the number of stages.

Figure 6.10 shows a simplified turbogenerator diagram. The turbine has two sections; extraction steam is discharged from the first section and exhaust steam from the second. Thus, as indicated on the diagram, there are three steam flows. The required analog inputs for the calculations are also indicated in the figure.

The turbogenerator calculation is set up as shown in Table 6.2. The first operation (STM) is used to calculate the properties of the throttle steam, flow 7 in Fig. 6.10. STM calculates the enthalpy, entropy, and specific volume of the throttle steam characterized by analog inputs 1 and 2. Operations 2 and 3, which characterize the extraction steam and the exhaust steam, are also STM. Operation 4,

TABLE 6.2

Turbogenerator Calculations[a]

Operation		User data element for storage (enthalpy)	Index (TTIII) for steam pressure	Index (TTIII) for steam temperature	User data index of entropy
Number	Code				
1	STM	TG No. 1 throttle steam	*XXX* psia	*XXX* °F	—
2	STM	TG No. 1 ext. steam	*XXX* psia	*XXX* °F	—
3	STM	TG No. 1 exh. steam	*XXX* psia	*XXX* °F	—
4	ISE	TG No. 1 ext. (ISEN)	*XXX* psia	—	*XXX* Btu/lb°F
5	ISE	TG No. 1 exh. steam	—	*XXX* °F	*XXX* Btu/lb°F
6	TUR[b]	TG No. 1 act. heat rate	—	—	—
7	END	—	—	—	—

[a] The calculation description is for TG No. 1, status is on, and execution group is 5–10 sec. From Blevins *et al.* (1980).

[b] Number of sections: 2.

ISE, is the isentropic expansion calculation for throttle steam through the first section. Enthalpy, steam temperature, and steam quality are computed from the inlet pressure and entropy. Similarly, Operation 5, ISE, is used for calculation of the isentropic expansion of the steam through the second section of the turbine. All data required for the two-section turbine calculation have now been prepared.

The sixth operation, TUR, calculates the turbine's actual heat rate, ideal heat rate, overall efficiency, mechanical efficiency, combined steam-path efficiency, and Sections 1 and 2 steam path efficiency. The arguments associated with the turbine command are contained in the specified data group shown in Table 6.3. When multiple results are calculated by an operation such as TUR, the results are stored sequentially in the database, starting with the specified data element for storage.

When analyzing the turbine–generator calculation presented in Table 6.3 it is important to recognize the modularity of the individual

TABLE 6.3
Turbogenerator Group Data for Unit No. 1, TG No. 1 Data

Element	Description	Type	Value
1	kW generated	Database location	*XXX* kW
2	Throttle steam flow	Database location	*XXX* lb/hr
3	Throttle steam (actual)	EM load/store no.	*XXX* lb/hr
4	Exhaust enthalpy (actual)	EM load/store no.	*XXX* Btu/lb
5	Exhaust enthalpy (ISEN)	EM load/store no.	*XXX* Btu/lb
6	Extraction 1 flow	Database location	*XXX* lb/hr
7	Extraction 1 enthalpy (actual)	EM load/store no.	*XXX* Btu/lb
8	Extraction 1 enthalpy (ISEN)	EM load/store no.	*XXX* Btu/lb

operations and how they can be combined to perform the required calculations. This modularity of function allows great flexibility in performing calculations for various types of turbines. The available operations can be combined to do the calculations for all turbines. This flexibility is an important design principle in the development of the energy management calculation package (EMCP).

3. TURBOGENATOR OPTIMIZATION

An optimizing tie-line control is required to minimize total electrical costs when tie-line and extraction–condensing turbogenerators are available to meet total plant electrical demand. To meet plant demand this control must choose between the available condensing turbogenerators and the utility tie-line. The IUCA technique discussed in Chapter 3 accomplishes this goal.

A functional diagram representing the application of the IUCA technique for tie-line control is shown in Fig. 6.11.

In tie-line control implementation the master demand variable is the integrated power demand over the utility company's demand period. Either a fixed or floating window technique can be used. A measured tie-line kilowatt load is preferred to the pulse-type meter indication. The master demand variable set point is set by the unit selector (US) function when the tie-line is the most economical choice for meeting the electrical system demand. The peak demand load must be its maximum limit. Configuration requirements include parameters and status calculations. The parameters are the electri-

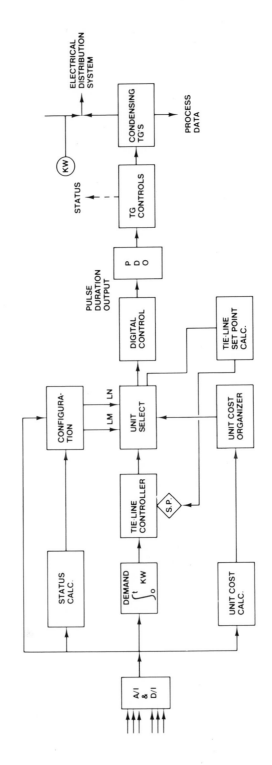

FIG. 6.11 Tie-line control using IUCA technique. (From Blevins *et al.*, 1980.)

cal load on turbogenerators and tie-lines, the throttle steam flow on turbogenerators, and the condensing steam flow on turbogenerators. Status considerations are the turbogenerators' control status, digital control loop status, and transmitter status.

Tie-line control allocation objectives are unit costs for generated electrical power and purchased electrical power. Purchased electrical power cost is based on utility contracts. Generated electrical costs are based on the efficiency of energy recovery from steam to electrical power, thence to heat. Units in selection are the loads on the condensing turbogenerators and set points for the utility tie-line. Digital control determines turbogenerator velocity limiting of speed–load set points and output through pulse-duration outputs to turbine controls. It also regulates high and low limiting on tie-line set points. Computer outputs are pulse-duration outputs to motorized speed–load pots on turbogenerators. There is no analog backup control; operators must manually load turbogenerators, unless the system is configured to have an automatic backup system.

The IUCA technique is an improved method of tie-line control. It establishes an optimum selection between condensing turbogenerators and tie-line loads that minimizes electrical cost. When demand is high and the tie-line is the least costly source of electrical energy, tie-line control will maintain the tie-line load at the utility demand limit, avoiding expensive demand charges.

If necessary, load shedding can be incorporated into the selection procedure. If the tie-line is at the demand limit and the condensing turbogenerators at their maximum generation capacity, the US could select a load-shedding route to maintain tie-line demand within limits.

For cogeneration facilities able to self-sufficiently meet their electrical energy demands, the tie-line control strategy shown in Fig. 6.11 can be modified to handle in-plant generation optimization. In this case, the tasks involved are optimum turbogenerator load allocation based on the condensing generation costs of each unit, extraction allocation based on section efficiency among the multiple-extraction turbines, and the possible inclusion of load-shedding strategy in the event of boiler and or turbogenerator shutdown.

It is not practical to consider all the possible turbogenerator configurations and operating constraints that exist in industrial plants. However, the calculation, optimization, and management procedures presented in this chapter should serve as a basis for tailoring systems to individual plant needs.

C. Cooling Towers (May, 1980)

Cooling-tower water is a critical utility for many process plants. The cooling-tower water is used for process cooling as well as condensing water in electrical power generation. The electrical cost for supplying cooling water to manufacturing or chemical processes can be a significant part of a plant's utility bill. Providing automatic control of the pump motors at the cooling towers is one way to reduce operating costs as much as 6–8%/year. There are a number of factors that make automatic pump control economically attractive. A small microprocessor-based computer system can be configured to handle the control logic and continuous control for cooling-tower optimization.

·1. COOLING-TOWER OPERATION

The heat load for a chemical process plant should remain fairly constant if the production rates are constant and the process is in an air-conditioned or well-enclosed environment. If the process vessels are located in an outside area, their ability to exchange heat will be affected by climatic conditions and seasonal weather changes. In this case, the total heat load required by the cooling tower servicing that process will vary considerably.

The number of pumps required at a cooling tower is determined by the process heat loads during the hottest, most humid weather. The full complement of pumps need be operated only during those periods of extreme weather conditions. Consequently, the kilowatt usage and subsequent operating costs should vary considerably with seasonal changes. If the electrical pumping costs in such a plant are approximately the same year-round, there is potential for cost reduction by the automation of pump control.

Cooling towers are frequently constructed in remote locations on the outer perimeters of plant sites and are not manned full time. In such cases, supply pumps, return pumps, and/or recirculation pumps are usually manually controlled by a roving operator making infrequent trips.

To handle unexpected peak loads caused by process needs it is necessary to keep one or more pumps running beyond the number actually required at the time of an operator's visit to the tower. Thus it can be seen that automatic pump control can often reduce pumping costs on a daily basis. Normal variations in process heat loads may require additional pumps at each tower to run only a few hours a day.

Turning pumps on and off can result in large variations in cooling-water pressure within the process area. These large changes in pressure make it difficult to tune local temperature-control loops for processes utilizing cooling water, thus keeping them in the automatic mode. The result may be that local controllers are placed in the manual mode and control valves moved to the full open position during a crisis condition when water pressure drops. Often, the process operators will be engaged in other activities at the time water pressure is restored and temperature controllers should be returned to automatic. Consequently, with this type of operation, more cooling water than is actually required will be recirculated. Providing for automatic header-pressure control for cooling water leaving the tower will allow process operators to keep local temperature controllers in the automatic mode yet ensure that adequate water is always available. The net result will be the reduction of pump running time and, therefore, operating costs.

2. ANALYSIS OF COOLING WATER REQUIRED

The cooling water required to service a given process depends on the process heat load, the amount and condition of each vessel's insulation, and the ambient wet-bulb temperature. Poorly insulated vessels will probably require less coolant during the winter months. It is difficult to estimate how changes in wet-bulb temperature affect each heat exchanger, but the effect of wet-bulb temperature changes at the tower can be calculated. As the ambient wet-bulb temperature decreases, the tower's ability to generate differential temperature between water leaving and water returning increases. The heat load seen by a cooling tower can be expressed as

$$\text{heat load} = (\Delta T) \times (FF), \qquad (6.10)$$

where ΔT is the difference in water temperature exiting and returning to the tower and FF the gallons per minute being pumped from and returned to the tower.

Thus if the heat load is assumed to be constant, increasing the ΔT at the tower will reduce the flow required for the heat load. Flow reduction can then be related to dollar savings by reducing the required number of pumps.

Typical design conditions supplied by a tower manufacturer may be a liquid–gas ratio (L/G) of 1.70, range equal to 12°F ΔT, wet-bulb temperature of 83°F, exit temperature of 90°F, and return temperature of 120°F. These design conditions can be used in conjunction with cooling-tower performance curves to determine how changes in the wet-bulb temperature affect the amount of flow required for the tower to service a given heat load. Table 6.4 shows the above design conditions when applied to the tower performance curves.

A plot of wet-bulb temperatures versus the number of pumps required, as well as the appropriate percentage of flows supplied by those pumps, is shown in Fig. 6.12.

Climatological data for 3 years prior to the present can be obtained from the local branch of the National Weather Bureau for any area surrounding a plant location. This information includes wet-bulb temperatures measured at 3-hour intervals for each day of the calendar year. From these listings, the wet-bulb temperature versus the total frequency of occurrences for each of the same calendar months over the 3-year period should be determined.

Cooling-tower performance curves, appropriate nomograms, and procedures for using the curves are available from the Cooling Tower Institute.

Table 6.5 depicts the complete listing of frequencies for a location in Florida during January of three consecutive years. The required

TABLE 6.4

Cooling-Tower Operating Conditions and Number of Pumps Required[a]

No. of supply pumps	Flow (%)	L/G	Wet-bulb temperature (°F)	Temperature range (°F)	Exit CWT (°F)	Return HWT (°F)
4	100	1.70	83	12	90	102
3	75	1.275	74	18	83	101
2	50	0.85	60	30	72	102
1	25	0.425	45	45	57	102

[a] From May (1980). © 1980 Technical Publishing, a company of the Dun and Bradstreet Corporation.

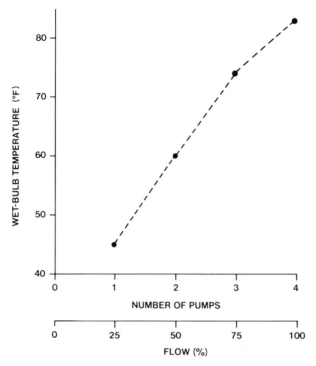

FIG. 6.12   Wet-bulb temperature versus number of pumps and percentage of flow.

number of pumps (as determined by Fig. 6.12) has been added to Table 6.5 for each range of wet-bulb temperature. Using data from this listing, the average number of pump hours required for a typical given calendar month can be determined as follows:

total average pump hours required, 1 calendar month

$$= \frac{\Sigma \; [\text{number of pumps} \times \text{total frequency}] \times \text{3-hour readings}}{\text{three sets of data for that calendar month}}.$$

(6.11)

For example, in a typical month of January, tower No. 4 required

$$\frac{[(1 \; \text{pump} \times 384) + (2 \times 252) + (3 \times 108)](\text{3-hr readings})}{\text{three sets of data for January}}$$

$$= 121 \; \text{pump hours}.$$

TABLE 6.5
Frequency Table for Wet-Bulb Temperature[a]

No. of pumps	Wet-bulb temp. (°F) from	Wet-bulb temp. (°F) to (not incl.)	Frequency	Total frequency	Percentage of total frequency	Cumulative percentage
1	9.00	10.00	1		0.13	0.13
	10.00	12.00	1		0.13	0.26
	12.00	14.00	1		0.13	0.39
	.	.	.		.	.
	.	.	.		.	.
	.	.	.		.	.
	40.00	42.00	46		6.18	41.80
	42.00	44.00	36		4.84	46.64
	44.00	46.00	37	384	4.97	51.61
2	46.00	48.00	26		3.49	55.11
	48.00	50.00	41		5.51	60.62
	.	.	.		.	.
	.	.	.		.	.
	.	.	.		.	.
	58.00	60.00	33		4.44	82.26
	60.00	62.00	24	252	3.23	85.48
3	62.00	64.00	37		4.97	90.46
	64.00	66.00	31		4.17	94.62
	.	.	.		.	.
	.	.	.		.	.
	.	.	.		.	.
	72.00	74.00	0		0.0	100.00
	74.00	76.00	0	108	0.0	100.00
4	76.00	78.00	0		0.0	100.00
	78.00	80.00	0		0.0	100.00
	80.00	82.00	0		0.0	100.00
	82.00	84.00	0		0.0	100.00
	84.00	86.00	0		0.0	100.00
	86.00	88.00	0		0.0	100.00
	88.00	90.00	0		0.0	100.00
Totals			744		100	

[a] From May (1980). © 1980 Technical Publishing, a company of the Dun and Bradstreet Corporation.

3. POTENTIAL COST SAVINGS

In an existing plant the potential savings to be gained by shutting down pumps more frequently can be calculated if one knows the current average running time for each pump on a monthly basis and the actual cost per kilowatt hour excluding fixed charges for peak power demand. This information may be obtained from accounting data, operating records, or maintenance records.

The electricity drawn by a motor can be approximated as

$$\text{electricity required (kW)} = \frac{(\text{horsepower})(746 \text{ W})}{1000 \times \text{motor efficiency}}. \quad (6.12)$$

The typical tower being discussed here utilizes four pumps producing 4500 gpm each and driven by 250-hp motors rated at 85% efficiency. If electrical costs are assumed to be $0.0300/kW·h, the cost of operating each motor is

$$\text{electricity required} = \frac{(250 \text{ hp}) \times (746 \text{ W})}{1000 \times 0.85} = 219.4 \text{ kW},$$

$$(219.4 \text{ kW}) \times (1 \text{ hr}) = 219.4 \text{ kW·h},$$

$$(219.4 \text{ kW·h}) \times (0.0300/\text{kW·h}) = \$6.58/\text{hr}.$$

Finally, potential cost savings per month can be developed as

$$\text{savings} = \left[\begin{array}{l} \text{total average} \\ \text{hours for a} \\ \text{given month with} \\ \text{pumps turned} \\ \text{on} \end{array} - \begin{array}{l} \text{total average} \\ \text{pump hours} \\ \text{required based} \\ \text{on wet-bulb} \\ \text{temperature} \\ \text{analysis} \end{array} \right] \left(\begin{array}{l} \text{cost per hour} \\ \text{for a} \\ \text{pump} \end{array} \right).$$

$$(6.13)$$

For example, if the motor running time reported for tower No. 1 averaged 2800 hours for January, and the analysis of cooling water required indicated that only 1212 pump hours were needed, then

$$\begin{array}{l} \text{potential savings} \\ \text{for January} \end{array} = [(2800 \text{ hr reported}) - (1212 \text{ hr required})]$$
$$\times \$6.58/\text{hr} = \$10,449.$$

A similar analysis should be run for each month of the year. Savings will naturally be greater during the winter months, but it is likely that this type of analysis will reveal a potential savings approaching $60,000/yr at each cooling tower.

This analysis should be done on the assumption that the heat load was constant in the most severe summer weather conditions. As previously stated, poorly insulated vessels will probably require less coolant during the cooler months. Consequently, the total plant heat load should go down in the winter. This factor makes the potential savings even greater.

4. MOTOR PROTECTION

The cost reduction method discussed herein may be accomplished by cycling the pump motors on and off in a timely, sequential fashion to control the pressure of water leaving the tower. Cooling-tower pump motors generally range in size from 125 to 400 hp. The logic system used to control motors this size must be designed to provide adequate protection for the motors. Without sufficient protective logic, excessive control action could cause physical damage to the motors. Subsequent increases in maintenance and reductions in reliability would then offset the savings derived from reduced running time.

It is not necessary to provide pressure control to an exact psig. Most of the potential savings can be achieved by controlling a reasonable range of pressure. If adequate flow is provided from a tower when the header pressure is 51 psig, then limits might be established at, say, 50 and 55 psig. A motor would be turned on when pressure dropped below 50 psig and another motor turned off when pressure exceeded 55 psig.

When large motors are started the current required to bring the motor to full rpm can be as much as five times the normal running current. This excess current generates large amounts of heat within the motor windings. The heat must then be dissipated by the cooling fan located inside the motor housing. Consequently, the control program must include a minimum running time to allow for proper cooling. Typically, this minimum time might be 30 min. When these motors are turned off, they retain a certain amount of residual heat that must also be dissipated. Therefore, a minimum downtime of perhaps 10 min is desirable.

Another measure that should be taken to minimize control action is the provision of a specific lapse time over which limits must be continuously exceeded before action is taken. Typically, this dead time might be 5 min. Such a delay prevents motor action from occurring during sporadic, short-term variations in water usage. All of these set points, lapse times, and run times should be variables that can be easily changed by the personnel responsible for tower operation.

The control action should also be rotated between motors to minimize increased maintenance on each motor. For example, if motor "A" is turned on when low pressure occurs, motor "B" or "C" should be turned off when high pressure occurs. This feature requires automating more than one pump at each tower. Maximum flexibility can be achieved by automating at least one-half of the motors at each tower. The motors not automated can then be started manually as required to base-load the system to a pressure less than the required minimum. The automated pumps can then be used to bring the pressure to some value slightly more than the minimum desired.

The amount of change in the cooling-water header pressure caused by turning on a single pump depends on the number of other pumps already running, the current pressure on the header pipe, the pump's characteristic curve, and the condition of the pump. These factors are important in determining the range of pressure to be controlled. More important is the fact that these conditions change with process needs and the seasons of the year. During cooler weather there should be fewer pumps running. Consequently, the change in pressure resulting from turning on one pump will be greater. In that situation, the low- and high-limit set points must be set further apart. Ideally, set points should be established for each season to ensure that motor action occurs not more than one to three times per day.

The atmosphere surrounding a cooling tower is always heavily laden with water vapor that has escaped from the tower. As a result, motors located within that environment are always wet. If the motors are not totally enclosed, the windings become saturated with moisture when they are not running. Trying to start motors with wet windings can cause ground-fault conditions and result in serious damage to the motor.

This problem can be prevented by the automatic application of a small amount of heat to keep the windings dry when the motors are not running. One way to do this is to apply a low-level dc voltage to the motor winding when it is down.

Because the switching action of motor starter gear is relatively slow, time-delay relays are recommended for the circuits designed to change the voltage levels. These time-delay relays would ensure that the high-level ac and low-level dc voltages were totally isolated from each other at all times.

5. CONTROL LOGIC

The obvious conclusion to be drawn from the previous section is that the majority of the logic required for this type of control is necessary for the protection of the motors. To safeguard the motors the control logic requires that the operator adjust the range of pressure to be controlled and the controller scan the actual pressure and compare it to set points. If the pressure is above the high set point, the controller starts the clock for lapse time or delay. If the out-of-limit condition persists throughout the lapse time, the controller checks to see if a supply pump is available to be stopped. If a pump is available, the controller checks to see if its minimum run time is satisfied. If so, the controller shuts off a motor and applies the low-level dc voltage required to keep the windings dry. Finally, the controlling device rotates the control motors within the software to provide action with a different motor when the next action is required.

The action that must be taken when the pressure drops below the low set point is quite similar. If the lapse time is satisfied, a supply pump is available, and minimum downtime is satisfied, the controller turns off the dc heating voltage and applies ac voltage to turn the motor on. Again, the control motors are rotated within the software.

6. MOTOR STATUS

For the controlling device to properly select the right motor for control action, the current status of the motors must be known. The controlling device must know if the motor is already running (motors on automatic control may also be started or stopped manually); if the breaker is physically racked in (this indicates that the motor and breaker are physically there and not in some state of repair); and if the motor is in an overload or ground-fault condition (in which case, electrical repair must be completed before the motor can be started). The status of these conditions can best be determined by feeding digital inputs—from spare contacts within the switch gear of auxiliary relays installed for that purpose—to the controlling device.

If the water pumping system is a recirculating closed loop, control action affects only one pump motor at a time, but if the system includes supply and return pumps, there may be sump reservoirs for each involved. The water levels within these sumps must be equalized for proper tower operation. This can best be done by taking control action on both supply and return pumps. With this type of control the status checks within the logic system must be designed to ensure that there is at least one supply and one return pump motor satisfying all pertinent conditions before control action can be exercised. If the supply and return pump are both on the same electrical feeder, it is best to stagger the starting action between the two by 30 to 40 seconds. Otherwise, the combined excess current required for their start-up might temporarily overload the feeder, and one motor would fail to start.

7. MICROCOMPUTER APPLICATION

The logic system required to provide pump motor control has a multitude of discrete inputs, outputs, and time delays that can easily be provided by a programmable controller. There are distinct advantages to using a microcomputer instead. These advantages are cost accounting, centralized control, and communication of information.

For cost accounting microcomputers can be set up to take in analog signal inputs and do arithmetic calculations. Consequently, a cost accounting system can be established by feeding in flow measurements from user buildings and wattage measurements from tower motor circuits. Charging production areas for their actual usage provides an incentive for production supervisors to find means of further reducing operating costs.

To implement centralized control microcomputers can be located in suitable air-conditioned areas near each cooling tower. These computers can then each be linked to a centrally located computer by two pairs of telephone lines. Thus all towers can be monitored by a single operator at a remote location, which also minimizes wiring costs.

Communication of information may also be accomplished by the use of microcomputers. They allow the communication of a maximum amount of information to the centralized control point. It is essential that the operator responsible for the system be kept abreast of computer actions and their effect on tower operation.

The microcomputer can provide a printout designed to show the status of a cooling tower: water pressure (both high and low), pump status, accumulated total flow, minimum time, number of motor starts, etc. Other capabilities of this system include the communication of cost information around the plant, data storage, and special messages to indicate when motors go down because of power failures or when computer initialized action is not completed.

7

Refrigeration Management Systems

Refrigeration machines that produce chilled water are critical for process and space cooling in certain industrial processes, particularly the manufacture of synthetic fibers. This utility also constitutes a significant operating cost.

In recent years computer systems have been widely used to provide control and optimization of large, chilled-water generation facilities. Many of the chilled-water systems that were installed when energy costs were low did not receive adequate attention to instrumentation. Instrumentation upgrading is necessary to permit real-time visibility of machine efficiencies, heat-exchanger fouling rates, and overall system operating costs. The process computer provides continuous monitoring of all analog instruments for the detection of failure and alarms, cross-checking for instrument accuracy through trend analysis, and reduction of overall system costs by influencing machine loading through the use of chiller models.

A. Basic Operation of a Refrigeration Machine

Refrigeration, or the withdrawal of heat, may be accomplished by several means including vapor-compression systems, thermoelectric means, or gas-compression systems involving expansion or throttling. Mechanical compression systems using fluorocarbon vapor refrigerants are widely used in industry. One such system is the centrifugal refrigeration machine shown in Fig. 7.1.

The four basic components of this system are the compressor, condenser, expansion device, and evaporator or cooler. The water to be chilled enters the cooler (evaporator) tubes and is chilled by the transferal of its heat to the cold liquid refrigerant. This causes the refrigerant to boil, changing it to a vapor. The vapor then moves to the suction side of the compressor, is compressed, and flows to the condenser.

The compressor can be powered by a steam-turbine or an electrical drive. Cooling water from either a nearby river or a cooling tower enters the condenser and removes the heat load from the

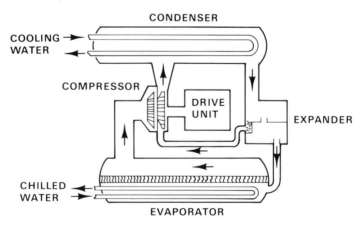

FIG. 7.1   Centrifugal refrigeration machine. (From May *et al.*, 1979.)

vapor refrigerant. Thus, the refrigerant is changed to a liquid again and flows to an expansion device (economizer) where its pressure and temperature are reduced to those in the cooler (evaporator). The refrigeration cycle is continuous.

A typical use of refrigeration machines is shown in Fig. 7.2. Plant users return up to 25,000 gpm of chilled water at 55 to 58°F. Several chilled-water supply pumps circulate this returned water through the set of refrigeration units, which cool the water to 48 to 50°F. Although the basic refrigeration cycles are similar, there is a wide variation in refrigerants (freon 11 and freon 12) and in types of drives (back-pressure, steam-turbine, and constant-speed motor drives). Individual machines may be controlled by turbine speed, suction-damper position, or inlet-vane position.

To ensure the adequate cooling capacity of the plant a pressure-control system regulates the amount of chilled water required. Because the plant's cooling load depends on ambient weather factors, the operators try to be generous in their estimates of the amount of chilled water needed so that a more than adequate supply is on-line to handle changing loads.

B. System Objectives

Even the most conscientious operating personnel cannot be expected to affectively maintain minimum operating costs unless there is adequate instrumentation for good visibility. The existing instrumentation in most plants is usually not sufficient to permit real-time performance monitoring of individual machine efficiencies and costs. Nor is there sufficient visibility to effectively adjust operating procedures as performance is changed by condenser or evaporator fouling, wear and tear of the drives, etc.

A number of chiller-system functions can be performed by a real-time, sensor-based computer. These include performing efficiency calculations, calculating unit operating costs, monitoring fouling characteristics, performing instrument-integrity checks and alarming when instruments exceed normal operating ranges, determining equipment deviations from normal operating ranges, accumulating data for engineering and accounting purposes, and allocating loads by maximum utilization of the least-costly refrigeration units needed

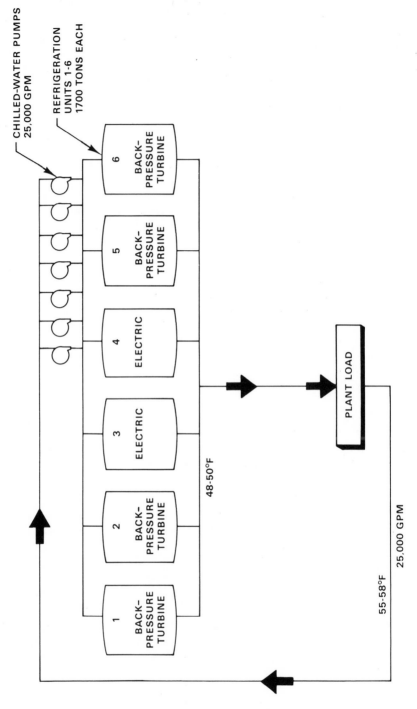

FIG. 7.2 Chilled-water system. (From May et al., 1979.)

to supply a plant load. These methods and techniques can be applied to many types of chiller systems whether they are mechanical, absorption, or centrifugal and whether they have steam or electric drives.

1. MEASUREMENT AND CALCULATIONS REQUIRED TO MANAGE THE SYSTEM

As shown in Fig. 7-3, the nine analog signals necessary for efficiency and cost calculations are chilled-water flow M_e, evaporator temperature differential ΔT_e, steam flow to turbine Q_s, steam tem-

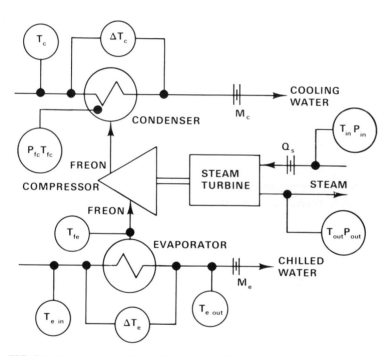

FIG. 7.3   Measurements for chiller machine. T_c, temperature of condensing water; ΔT_c, temperature difference across the condenser; M_c, condensing water flow; P_{fc}, condenser freon pressure; T_{fc}, condenser freon temperature; T_{fe}, evaporator freon temperature; $T_{e\,in}$, temperature of chilled-water inlet; $T_{e\,out}$, temperature of chilled-water outlet; ΔT_e, temperature difference across the evaporator; M_e, chilled-water flow; T_{in}, inlet steam temperature; P_{in}, inlet steam pressure; T_{out}, outlet steam temperature; P_{out}, outlet steam pressure; Q_s, steam flow. (From May *et al.*, 1979.)

perature in T_{in}, steam pressure in P_{in}, steam pressure out P_{out}, steam temperature out T_{out}, cooling-water flow M_c, and condenser temperature differential ΔT_c.

Several arbitrary terms are used to express the performance of a refrigeration cycle. A ton of refrigeration is the refrigeration produced by melting one ton of ice at a temperature of 32°F in 24 hr. This is equivalent to a heat withdrawal rate of 12,000 Btu/hr. Thus the capacity of a given refrigeration machine expressed in tons would be

$$\text{load} = C_p M_e (\Delta T_e)/12{,}000, \qquad (7.1)$$

where load is the machine load in tons, C_p the specific heat of water in Btu's per pound degrees Farenheit, M_e the mass flow rate of water in the evaporator in pounds per hour, and ΔT_e the temperature differential measured across the evaporator in degrees Farenheit. Referring to Fig. 7.3, the relative positions of these measurements are noted as M_e and ΔT_e.

The work of compression, or energy supplied to the refrigeration machine by the prime mover, is calculated as

$$W_s = Q_s \, \Delta h_s \qquad \text{for} \quad \text{steam drive units}, \qquad (7.2)$$

where W_s is the compressor-supplied energy in Btu's per hour, Q_s the mass flow rate of steam in pounds per hour, and Δh_s the enthalpy change of steam across the turbine in Btu's per pound. The positions of these measurements in Fig. 7.3 are noted as $T_{in}P_{in}$, $T_{out}P_{out}$, and Q_s.

The effectiveness of a refrigeration system is usually expressed by the coefficient of performance (COP) and is defined by the dimensionless equation

$$\text{COP} = \frac{\text{useful refrigeration effect}}{\text{net energy supplied by external sources}}$$

or

$$\text{COP} = \frac{\text{load} \times 12{,}000}{W_s}.$$

Another useful form of the equation is

$$\text{COP} = \frac{12{,}000}{2545 \times (\text{hp/ton})} = \frac{4.72}{\text{hp/ton}}. \qquad (7.3)$$

The total costs of operating a unit in the system can be expressed as

$$\text{cost} = K_c \times W_s + \frac{K_e \times M_e}{\rho_e} + \frac{K_p \times M_c}{\rho_c}, \qquad (7.4)$$

where cost is the cost of operating in dollars per hour, K_c the compressor input energy cost factor in dollars per Btu or dollars per kilowatt-hour, W_s the compressor work in Btu's per hour or kilowatt-hour, K_e the pumping cost factor for chilled water in dollars per gallon, M_e the mass flow rate of chilled water in pounds per hour, ρ_e the density of chilled water in pounds per gallon, K_p the pumping cost factor for condenser cooling water in dollars per gallon, M_c the mass flow rate of condenser cooling water in pounds per hour, and ρ_c the density of condenser water in pounds per gallon.

2. MEASUREMENTS NEEDED FOR INSTRUMENT INTEGRITY CHECKS

Measurement of the temperature differential across the heat exchangers shown in Fig. 7.3 is a potential problem and care should be considered when selecting the measuring elements. First, a matched pair of resistance-type temperature bulbs with an accuracy of 0.1°F is needed to provide the necessary accuracy for the heat-balance and instrument-integrity calculations. Second, since the measurement bulbs will be operating at a temperature below the dew point, the seal at the top of the bulb must be of a superior quality or condensate will form inside the measuring element and affect its accuracy.

For any system to provide accurate information on which to base operating decisions, it needs certain automatic and continuous checks to ensure the integrity and validity of the instrument signals. There are basically two types of checks: heat-balance calculation and deviation trend alarming on specific signals.

A heat-balance check calculates the ratio of the rejected heat energy to the energy input to the system. The energy rejected in a refrigeration machine is the condenser heat load. The energy input is the sum of the compressor work [calculated from Eq. (7.2)] and the evaporator heat load [calculated by Eq. (7.1)].

TABLE 7.1
Example of a Refrigeration Chiller Report[a]

Parameters	Unit	Parameters	Unit	Parameters	Unit
Comp. (mb/hr)	3.63	Cool. flow	1986.98	Cond. temp.	100.00
Evap. (mb/hr)	20.77	Cool. DT	24.28	Cond. U	298.24
Cond. (mb/hr)	24.15	Cool. in	53.00	Cond. FF	0.002844
% Out/in	98.94	COP	5.71	Cycle. eff.	73.03
Load (T)	1731.48	Chill. DT	10.23	Evap. temp.	36.57
Hp/ton	0.024850	Chill. out	45.67	Evap. U	495.39
Turb eff.	Electric	Chill. flow	4056.46	Evap. FF	0.000290
$/Ton-day	0.463635	Cond. leak	1.06	Cond. HD	7.50
Run time this shift: 282 min					

[a] Report is taken per unit per day per time. From May *et al.* (1979).

If all analog signals are accurate and there are no significant thermal losses in the cycle, the resultant ratio should be 100. For example, Table 7.1 shows a heat balance (% out/in) of 98.94 for the day shown. The heat-balance check is extremely useful in locating erroneous or inaccurate instrument signals.

The computer should make use of extensive trend alarming on critical signals such as the one for chilled-water temperatures. By summing the temperature differential across the evaporator (ΔT_e) and the outlet temperature ($T_{e\,out}$) and comparing this with the temperature inlet to the evaporator ($T_{e\,in}$), a check can be made of the relative accuracy of the temperature instruments. If these values exceed a specified percentage difference, then a trend-alarm message can be printed out.

Another type of trend alarm sums the flows from all the individual machines that empty into a common header and compares their collective flow to the total flow measurement. If these two values exceed a specified percentage, then a message can be printed out for the instrument mechanic.

3. MEASUREMENTS NEEDED FOR OTHER PERFORMANCE CHARACTERISTICS

To assist the engineer and operating personnel in troubleshooting a unit, several other performance characteristics should be computed. Two examples where this type of checking can be beneficial are the detection of air leakage in the evaporator and the determination of heat exchanger fouling rates.

Air leakage into the evaporator depresses the partial pressure of the refrigerant. This means a higher pressure is required to condense it. Air leakage can be monitored by measuring the pressure and temperature of the refrigerant leaving the condenser. The ratio of the refrigerant-saturated vapor pressure at the measured temperature (T_{fc}) to the measured pressure (P_{fc}) can indicate air leakage. If this ratio is substantially less than unity, then leakage is indicated and appropriate corrective action should be taken (see Fig. 7.3).

Perhaps the most crucial performance characteristic of refrigeration machines is the fouling rate of the condenser heat exchanger. Fouling is caused by the deposition of sediment, scale, or biological growth on the water side of tubes. This results in increased condenser pressures and, consequently, increased power requirements for the compressor.

Figure 7.4 is a profile of a fouled heat-transfer surface. Fouling resistance is determined from the overall heat-transfer coefficient of the fouled and initial (clean) conditions, or

$$\text{fouling factor} = 1/U_f - 1/U_i$$

and

$$U_f = Q/A \times \Theta_m, \qquad (7.5)$$

where Q is the condenser heat load in Btu's per hour, A the con-

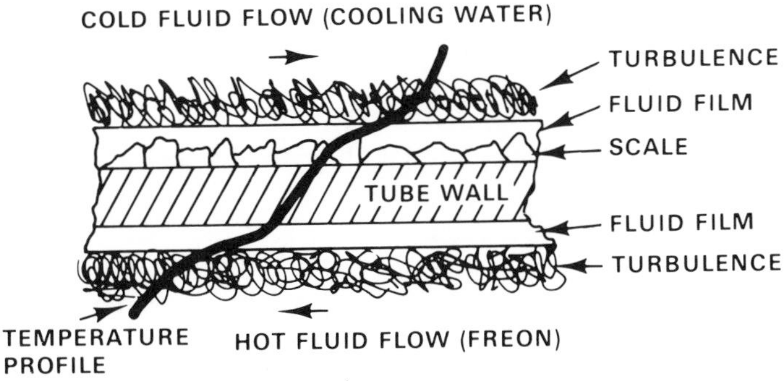

FIG. 7.4   Profile of heat-transfer section in the condenser section.

denser surface area in square feet, and Θ_m the log-mean temperature difference.

Because Θ_m is a function of flow, a model is needed to permit the calculation of U_i at the same condenser load at which U_f is being calculated.

Working from standard equations describing the overall heat-transfer coefficients and assuming that fouling occurs only on the side of the tube for the cooling fluid, the heat-transfer surface areas are equal, and certain terms in the equations can be lumped into a constant so an area correction is not needed, an expression can be developed for U_i as

$$\frac{1}{U_i} = \frac{1}{U_d} - \frac{1}{h_f} - \frac{1}{h_s} + \frac{1}{h_f \left(\dfrac{\text{condenser flow}_{\text{actual}}}{\text{condenser flow}_{\text{design}}}\right)^{0.85}}, \qquad (7.6)$$

where U_d is Eq. (7.5) evaluated at design conditions, h_f the convective heat-transfer film coefficient evaluated at design conditions and equal to the equation $163V^{0.85} (1 + 0.0104T)$, where V is the water velocity through the tubes in feet per second, T the average inside and outside tube temperature in degrees Farenheit, and h_s the scale heat-transfer coefficient at design (the accepted industry standard is 2000).

By periodically evaluating Eqs. (7.5) and (7.6) and storing the results in the computer, the fouling rate of the condenser surface may be evaluated. This continuous checking of the fouling rate will allow better scheduling of maintenance to clean the condensers, thus reducing the costs of operation.

4. MEASUREMENTS NEEDED FOR LOAD-ALLOCATION MODELS (Zimmer, 1975)

The performance of a centrifugal refrigeration machine is a function of seven variables: chilled-water flow through the evaporator, differential temperature across the evaporator, chilled-water inlet temperature, water flow through the condenser, differential temperature across the condenser, condenser-water inlet temperature, and condenser freon pressure. Thus one can write an equation of the form shown below to represent the efficiency performance characteristics of a refrigeration machine:

$$\text{HP} = f(M_e, \Delta T_{e\,in}, M_c, \Delta T_c, T_{c\,in}, P_{fc}). \qquad (7.7)$$

The exact relationships and interactions of these seven variables may not be known even by manufacturers, so a carefully designed test should be developed to run each machine over a selected range of its variables to collect the data necessary for the model. As many as 100 data points per machine may be required to develop the models. A typical model is

$$Y = A + (B \times x_1) + (C \times x_2) + (D \times x_3) + (E \times x_4) + (F \times x_5), \qquad (7.8)$$

where Y is the compressor required horsepower, A is a constant from the regression (fitting) program, B, C, D, E, F are fitted coefficients, $x_1, \ldots, x_5$ state variables obtained through statistical analysis and described as

$$x_1 = \left(\frac{M_e \times \Delta Te}{24000}\right) - \bar{x}_1,$$

where $\bar{x}_1$ is the arithmetic average of x_1;

$$x_2 = \left(\frac{M_c \times \Delta T_c}{24,000} - \frac{M_e \times \Delta T_e}{24,000}\right) \times 100 - \bar{x}_2,$$

where $\bar{x}_2$ is the average of x_2;

$$x_3 = (T_{e\,in} - \tfrac{1}{2}\Delta T_e) - \bar{x}_3,$$

where $\bar{x}_3$ is the average of x_3;

$$x_4 = (\alpha/\sqrt{P_{fc}}) - \bar{x}_4,$$

where $\bar{x}_4$ is the average of x_4 and α the mean value for condenser head pressure;

$$x_5 = (T_c + \tfrac{1}{2}\Delta T_c) - \bar{x}_5,$$

where $\bar{x}_5$ is the average of x_5. (See Fig. 7.3 for symbols.)

Figure 7.5 shows typical performance curves generated from the models of six refrigeration machines. Once the models have been determined, coefficients A_i–F_i are manually fed into the on-line control computer for each chiller. These models are periodically compared on-line against current performance. When the predicted compressor work consistently exceeds limits of acceptability from the

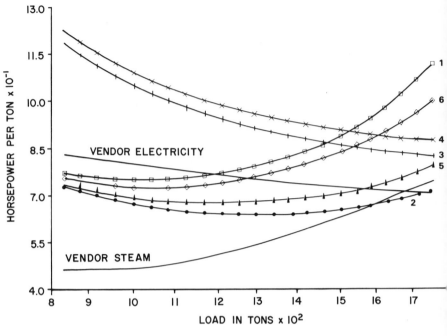

FIG. 7.5   Efficiency versus load.

current performance, the models can be updated using the same procedure.

5. APPLICATION OF NELDER–MEAD
OPTIMIZER FOR LOAD ALLOCATION
THROUGH SUPERVISORY CONTROL

The large capacity of many installed plant chiller systems usually results in the partial loading of some machines during several months of the year. Partial loading is the key to load allocation or optimization. The suggestions of machine load allocations are based on real-time performance calculations to minimize the total costs.

The flowchart of the optimization procedure is shown in Fig. 7.6. The chart shows that the optimizer can be activated through manual request by an operator or by an incremental plant load change of some value. At the time of optimizer request, a number of automatic

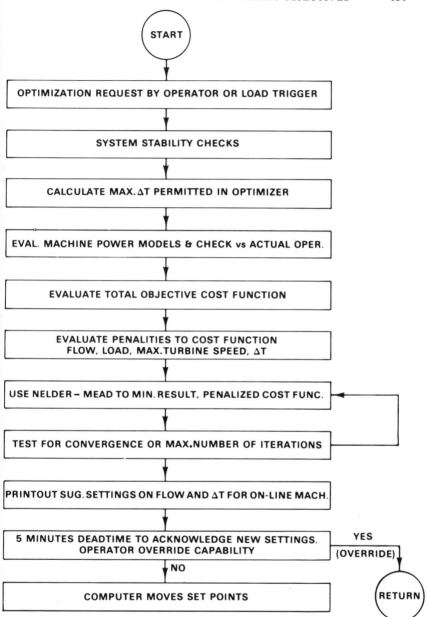

FIG. 7.6   Flowchart of optimizer procedure.

system checks of freon temperature, temperature of water going to the plant, operating pressure, and maximum–minimum flow are made to ensure stable operating conditions exist for optimization. If stable conditions exist, then the total objective-cost function is evaluated prior to analysis by the Nelder–Mead Simplex method.

The objective function (total system operating cost) can be rewritten as

$$C_T = \sum_{i=1}^{n} (C_p + C_a + C_b)_i, \qquad (7.9)$$

where C_T is the operating cost in dollars per hour, C_p the operating cost associated with the prime mover, C_a the cost associated with chilled-water pumping, and C_b the cost associated with condenser-water pumping (in this case river water is used for condenser cooling water).

Load allocation seeks to minimize the cost function shown in Eq. (7.9) subject to the following constraints:

$$\sum_{i=1}^{n} \text{load}_i = \text{total demand load}, \qquad (7.10)$$

$$\text{load}_i \leq \text{maximum load for chillers}_i, \qquad (7.11)$$

$$\max \Delta T_i \leq f(x), \qquad (7.12)$$

where x may be operating conditions, minimum set point by operator, or predicted turbine speed.

The method used to solve for the overall minimum system cost is a custom version of the Nelder–Mead Simplex method for function minimization. The routine seeks to minimize a function of several variables N by comparing the values of the function at $N + 1$ points of a simplex. This method is appealing because the absence of derivatives makes it computationally very economical.

The Nelder–Mead method's initial return is an evaluation of the objective function Eq. (7.9) at the current operating conditions. Then each parameter, in this case the chilled-water flow and the ΔT_e across the evaporator, is perturbed by an arbitrary step size, and the object function is evaluated at each point.

The method was originally intended for use without constraints but has been modified to handle constraints through the use of penalty functions. Examples of some constraints are minimum or maximum chilled-water flows, temperature, maximum turbine speed, and maximum loads. Whenever a constraint is violated, the effect on the objective-cost function is increased by the square of the violation. This speeds the processing time required and forces the function back within acceptable ranges. The number of functional evaluations required for convergence is roughly proportional to the square of the number of variables.

After the minimum system cost within the constraints has been found, the computer prints out an optimization log containing the current machine settings and the suggested machine settings. Table 7.2 shows an example of one such printout for the case when three refrigeration units are being run. In this case, the optimizer recommends increasing the temperature differential across the evaporator and lowering the water flow. If the pumping costs were not considered and the objective cost functions were based solely on the prime-mover costs, the suggested settings would recommend reducing the temperature differential and increasing the flow. Obviously, the actual savings depend on the distance of the actual figures from the initial optimum points and on the number of chillers being optimized.

After the log shown in Table 7.2 has been printed, a time lag of 5 min is permitted to allow for operator override of the recommenda-

TABLE 7.2

Example of Optimization Results[a]

		Current			Suggested		
			Change in			Change in	
Unit	Status	Flow	temp.	Load (T)	Flow	temp.	Load (T)
1	Comp. control	3779.19	8.26	1303.47	2529.48	11.20	1181.93
2	Comp. control	3756.45	8.55	1341.02	2535.23	11.20	1185.20
3	Off	0.00	0.00	0.00	0.00	0.00	0.00
4	Off	0.00	0.00	0.00	0.00	0.00	0.00
5	Comp. control	3728.44	6.30	981.17	2712.18	11.12	1258.54
6	Off	0.00	0.00	0.00	0.00	0.00	0.00
7	Idle	0.00	0.00	0.00	0.00	0.00	0.00
8	Idle	0.00	0.00	0.00	0.00	0.00	0.00

[a] Chiller operating costs: optimum loads cost ($/hr), 28.40; preoptimization cost ($/hr), 31.78; adjusted savings ($/day), 81.12; equal loads cost ($/hr), 28.31; number of evaluations, 73; optimization began at 14:06 and ended at 14:12.

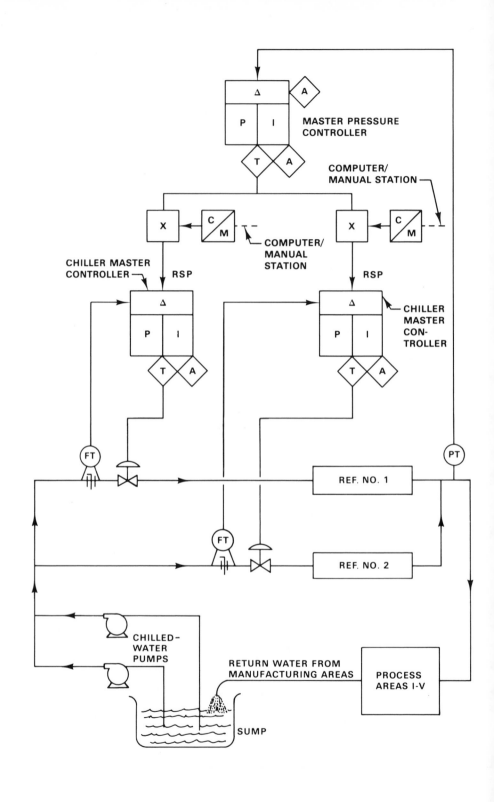

tions. If the operator does not acknowledge, the computer then pulses the controllers to the new set points by a control algorithm. This algorithm for each flow and ΔT_e control loop contains ramp control and may be adjusted for frequency of pulsing and number of pulses per period.

C. Implementation of Management Systems

So far we have presented all of the elements that are necessary prerequisites to the implementation of a chiller management system. A management system should be selected and configured to provide data acquisition, calculations, and control and the execution of optimization routines. In addition it should provide logs, alarms, and display functions for operating information.

In recent years most computer-based chiller management systems installed were minicomputer-based systems, either operating in direct digital control or supervisory control modes. One example discussed in this chapter is a supervisory control scheme in which the local control system is implemented with analog controllers and a minicomputer system providing a set of optimum set points to both the chilled-water temperature and flow controllers. The recent introduction of distributed control systems allows a distributed hierarchical control system to be configured to handle the same management tasks outlined in this chapter. The lowest-level control functions can be performed by microprocessor-based controllers that communicate to a host computer via a data highway.

1. A FLEXIBLE CONTROL SCHEME

Sometimes the operating constraints inherent in a particular process necessitate designing maximum flexibility into its control scheme. Figures 7.7 and 7.8 show an example of a control scheme that offers a multitude of options to the operator. This particular example illustrates the methods of controlling the flow of water through two refrigeration machines. The output from the master pressure controller (MPC) is used to change the set points of individ-

FIG. 7.7   Automatic allocation of chiller load. (From May *et al.*, 1979.)

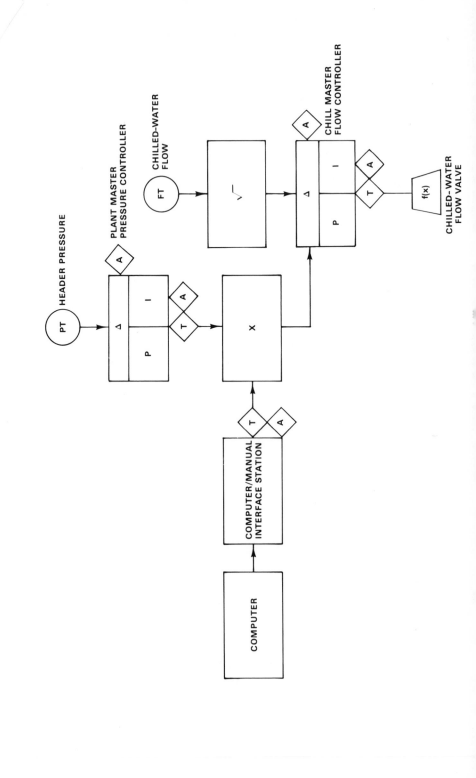

ual flow controllers (i.e., chiller master controller) to control the flow of water through each machine. Before it reaches each flow controller the signal from the MPC is fed through multiplier modules. The other input to the multiplier module comes from the manual-bias stations. With this arrangement, an operator can manually bias one machine to carry more or less flow than another, while the overall system still maintains control of the water pressure (see Fig. 7.7).

2. INTERFACING TO THE COMPUTER

The manual-bias station shown in Fig. 7.7 also contains a digital-to-analog converter. This is the component used to interface the control system to the computer. The computer can be used to calculate the multiplier factors required for the biasing to redistribute the load and the number of pulses required to change the multiplier factors from existing to new values. Consequently, the computer can be effectively used to determine the optimum flow settings and to implement load distribution accordingly.

Interfacing an analog control system to the computer in this manner has two distinct advantages. First, the operation of the process is not dependent on the computer. The instantaneous control of the process is handled by the analog control system. Therefore the control of the machines can be taken away from the computer at any time. This approach adds flexibility yet keeps the interface simple. Second, a failure of any part of the computer will not cause an upset in the control of the process. A specific number of positive or negative pulses is required to drive the output up or down from the bias station. When failures occur within the computer hardware or software, no new pulses are generated. Therefore, the outputs of the bias stations will remain as they were before the computer failure.

D. System Benefits

The reasons for the application of an energy management system to the refrigeration plant include improved transient response and control-loop stability in response to load changes, improved day-to-

TABLE 7.3

Energy Reductions in the Variable Costs for a Textile Plant—a Case History

	Base		
Utilities	1976	1979	% Change
Steam usage			
(MBtu/ton-day)	0.10	0.08	−20
Electrical usage			
(kWh/ton-day)	8.43	7.00	−17
River water usage			
(kgal/ton-day)	3.11	2.38	−23
Cooling water usage			
(kgal/ton-day)	1.14	1.12	−2
Total net energy			
(MBtu/ton-day)	0.25	0.22	−12.5

day operation permitted by the current real-time visibility of machine parameters, reduced operational costs through optimum load allocation, and better scheduling of maintenance programs.

This author is personally acquainted with an installation in which a dedicated minicomputer system has been in operation for the past 7 years in a chiller complex similar to the one shown in Fig. 7.2. Table 7.3 shows details of the unit energy reductions in the variable costs between 1976 and 1979, using 1976 as a base year. The total incremental energy required to generate refrigeration has decreased by over 12% (on a unit energy per ton-day basis) with no substantial change in plant cooling loads (Cho and Norden, 1979).

8

Energy Accounting and System Diagnostics

In recent years energy accounting has been viewed as a vital, integral part of computer-based energy management systems. To evaluate the energy-utilization efficiency of the plant, e.g., boilers, turbogenerators, compressors, and chillers as well as various process unit operations, it is important to measure energy delivered to the point of users as accurately as possible.

Real-time information and historical data on energy consumption rates should be distributed among the users so that optimum energy distribution strategies can be developed. Energy accounting systems also allow utility engineers to track and correct any abnormal imbalances between energy suppliers and users.

A computer-based energy accounting system may include the following specific functions:

(1) on-line energy balance of steam, electricity, compressed air, and chiller and plant water (Steam leakage can be detected and appropriate actions can be taken.);

(2) development of energy standards for each of the cost centers, e.g., the ratio of the finished or in-process product to the energies consumed (The computer should monitor and report any deviations from the established standards.);

(3) evaluation of the efficiency of steam-load allocations with respect to their work and heat content on a plantwide basis;

(4) plans for future energy utilization policies and strategies using historical energy data;

(5) management of contracted purchased energies such as natural gas (Management may include decisions such as when to switch over to expensive backup fuels, e.g., No. 6 oil or propane gas.).

A. Utility Accounting

A number of selected utility accounting systems and their objectives and functions are presented in this section.

1. STEAM METERING

Steam metering requirements are quite similar in most plants. Steam data, both in pounds per hour and Btu's per hour, are logged and totalized at, for example, 8-hr and 24-hr intervals. The ambitious steam metering programs strive toward a 2–3% steam balance by proper selection, installation, calibration, and maintenance of a sensor and transmitter.

The applications of the computer system may include steam metering by a product or cost center, log steam energy utilization improvement based on equipment changes or changes in the mode of operation, and improved control. To enhance steam metering accuracy, a number of factors must be carefully evaluated.

The basic equation of compressible gas flow is

$$Q = \frac{SC_d Y_a A \sqrt{\rho_b} \sqrt{\Delta P} \sqrt{\rho_a/P_b}}{\sqrt{1 - B^4}}, \qquad (8.1)$$

where Q is the flow rate in pounds per hour, A the pipe cross-sectional area in square inches, ΔP the differential pressure across the orifice in pounds per square inch, and P_b the downstream steam pressure, ρ_a steam density upstream in pounds per cubic inch, ρ_b steam density downstream in pounds per cubic inch, S the scale factor, C_d the discharge coefficient, Y_a the adiabatic expansion factor, and $B = d_1/d_2$, where d_1 is the diameter of the orifice in inches and d_2 the diameter of the pipe in inches.

Equation (8.1) clearly indicates that there are a number of factors that are functions of the fluid properties and physical dimensions of the metering device. Therefore the accuracy of the metering device depends on how closely the variables can be measured and introduced into Eq. (8.1) for calculation. Furthermore, the application guidelines of the device (e.g., range, turndown ratio, and temperature of fluid) should not be violated.

In some cases the computer system is extensively used in the application of Eq. (8.1) by determining C_d as a function of the Reynolds number (i.e., having the individually calibrated C_d versus the Reynolds number stored in the computer, Y_a as a function of specific heat ratio including inlet specific weight of steam. Also, all metered flows are pressure and temperature compensated.

Steam metering algorithms include mass-flow calculations based on filtered-pressure, temperature, differential-pressure signals, and other variables mentioned in Eq. (8.1). The calculated mass-flow rate is usually integrated for shift and daily logs and stored for trending. Btu's are calculated using the corrected mass flow multiplied by the enthalpy of the steam. They are also integrated for shift and daily logs and stored for trending and accounting purposes.

2. ELECTRICAL METERING

The objective of electrical metering is similar, in most cases, to that of steam metering. The computer system may be used to

(1) obtain accurate metering of electrical loading from all generating sources (including purchased kilowatts) and from all major users of electrical power,
(2) monitor frequency, voltage, and megavars at critical points on the high-voltage electrical distribution system,

(3) monitor the operation of critical breakers and critical loads of the high-voltage electrical distribution system, and

(4) report both kilowatt-hours and Btu's on an 8- and 24-hr basis.

The acquisition of electrical data allows the operating personnel to track fully a detailed description of the electrical-distribution system for the purpose of evaluating it during normal, and especially during abnormal, conditions. Electrical metering and monitoring allow evaluation of the electrical energy requirements of products, electrical energy savings due to equipment changes, and electrical energy improvement based on a change in the mode of operation.

The system algorithm may include the status of all load breakers, tie breakers, and electrical Btu's balanced by readily accessible means such as special-function pushbuttons. Control of the generator load may be achieved by changing the set point of the generator designated to pick up the load.

3. RECOVERING CONDENSATE

Quality monitoring is essential in condensate recovery because process leaks can contaminate the condensate. The basic approach may include defining all sources of condensate being returned, establishing which chemicals from each source can contaminate the condensate, developing indices for condensate quality, and developing a plan to manage the condensate-collection system. This approach should ensure that each process unit or building returns as much condensate as possible when the quality is acceptable.

A program for recovering and dumping condensate can be developed for each of the process units or buildings, as shown in Fig. 8.1. If the chemical that each unit or building contributes to the contamination of the condensate is identified, then it is not difficult to establish the index (or indices) for monitoring condensate quality. Analyzers to measure conductivity, total carbon, pH, and iron concentration should be installed. These should monitor and initiate automatic dumping of the condensate via a three-way valve if it is contaminated and exceeds the set point under computer control.

Cost savings can be easily calculated once the net increase in the condensate return has been determined. Three basic factors are re-

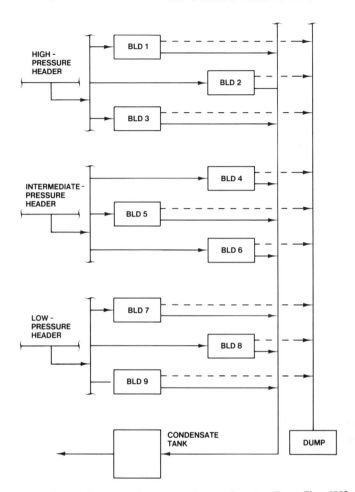

FIG. 8.1   System for recovering or dumping condensate. (From Cho, 1982a.)

lated to the value of the steam condensate: energy of condensate above energy of makeup water, cost of equivalent purchased water, and cost of chemical treatment. Consider the following example. For a plant with an average steam demand of 350,000 lb/hr, in which the average percentage of condensate recovered was 45% before installation of monitors and 70% afterward, the temperature of the returned condensate is 200°F. The temperature of the makeup water is 60°F, the boiler fuel costs are $4/MBtu, the cost of equivalent purchased water is $0.02/1000 lb, chemical treatment costs $0.08/1000 lb, and boiler efficiency is 0.80.

Energy savings are as follow: net increase in condensate return is 87,500 lb/hr, energy saved per pound of condensate is 175 Btu/lb, total energy savings are 15.31 MBtu/hr, fuel-cost savings are ($15.31)(4)(8000) = $489,920/yr, chemical savings are (87,500)(0.08/1000)(8000) = $56,000/yr, and the water savings are (87,500)(0.02/1000)(8000) = $14,000/yr. The total cost savings are $559,920 per year.

4. WORK AND HEAT ACCOUNTING

In most industrial plants the steam is distributed to different users through steam headers having different levels of pressure and temperature. As the steam changes in state from high to low pressure and temperature, its quality, i.e., available work, degrades. Therefore, the steam distribution and allocation strategy should be based on maximizing the use of available work while satisfying the heat requirements of process operations. The available work for each condition can be determined by inserting the steam properties into Eq. (8.2):

$$W_a = T_0 \Delta S_R - \Delta H, \tag{8.2}$$

where W_a is the available work in Btu's per pound, T_0 the ambient reference temperature (520°R), ΔS_R the entropy changes in Btu's per pound degrees Farenheit, and ΔH the change in enthalpy in the steam in Btu's per pound.

Table 8.1 illustrates the available work for several typical steam conditions between the initial conditions and water at the reference of 60°F and entropy at 0.056 Btu/lb°F. Similarly, ΔH is the enthalpy change from initial conditions to water at 60°F and 28 Btu/lb. The last column in Table 8.1 clearly shows the decrease in percentage of available work as a ratio of W_a to ΔH.

The throttling process across the pressure-reducing valve (PRV) wastes available energy while conserving enthalpy. Therefore, it is very desirable to expand the steam through turbine drives to extract horsepower, while providing a lower-pressure steam to the distribution system.

TABLE 8.1
Available Work in Steam at Various Conditions[a]

Pressure (psia)	Temperature (°F)	Enthalpy (Btu/lb)	Entropy (Btu/lb °F)	W_a (Btu/lb)	$-W_a/\Delta H$ (%)
2500	1000	1458	1.527	665	46.5
1200	1000	1449	1.630	602	42.4
600	700[b]	1352	1.584	529	40.0
400	445[b]	1205	1.485	433	36.8
250	401[b]	1201	1.526	408	34.8
140	353[b]	1193	1.575	375	32.2
100	328[b]	1187	1.603	354	30.5
50	281[b]	1174	1.659	312	27.2
20	228[b]	1156	1.732	256	22.7

[a] From Shinskey (1978).
[b] Saturated.

B. Example of Steam Balance in a Pulp and Paper Mill

To develop a good understanding of steam balancing we shall make use of Fig. 8.2, which depicts a typical steam system in a pulp and paper mill. The equipment in this system was initially selected to satisfy the mill's energy requirements for the production of 1000 tons of pulp per day. These requirements are specified by the energy needs of the necessary equipment. The necessary process equipment includes digesters, paper and tissue machines, pulp dryers, evaporators, bleach, and caustics. The necessary powerhouse equipment consists of a deaerator, high- and low-pressure feedwater heaters, boiler feedwater pumps, induced-draft fans, soot-blowing equipment, and turbogenerators.

In general, the equipment used in the generation and distribution of steam is determined by the specific production objectives of the plant. Therefore, there is neither a standard system nor a standard steam balance for all plants.

The purpose of this example is to help the user analyze the steam balance in his plant and recognize the opportunities for maximizing the use of every pound of steam. These opportunities may involve

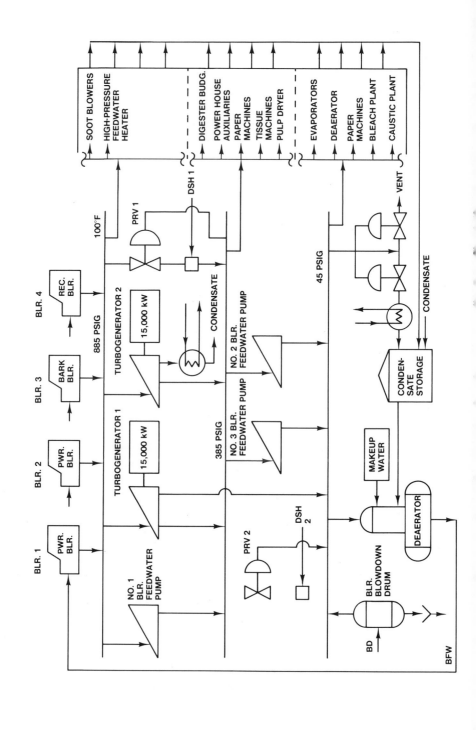

modification of operating policy, addition of capital equipment, re-evaluation and revamping of control systems in the steam distribution system, or additional recovery of condensate.

Before proceeding with an evaluation of the potential energy savings in our example, we need to determine the base-case steam balance. Then, by modifying this balance (without upsetting production) we can make cost comparisons between the base case and the alternatives.

The energy savings are the difference between the energy required in the base case and that required with the alternative steam allocation. The variables that determine the fuel cost for steam in the pulp and paper mill shown in Fig. 8.2 are boiler steam-generation costs (recovery boiler, bark boiler, power boilers), pressure–reduction-valve stations between steam-supply headers, in-plant generation of electricity, purchase of electricity, turbines for pumps and fans, 60-psia steam vent, 45-psia steam to deaerator, condensate return, makeup water, boiler feedwater, and unaccounted-for steam.

Close examination of the steam-use logs for the last 1–3 yr should reveal the amount of low-pressure steam venting. If excessive venting is correlated with seasonal variations in steam use or with expected fluctuations based on changes in production, steam cost can be reduced by finding low-pressure steam users or by adding turbine drives as an alternative to motor-driven plant auxiliaries. Table 8.2 shows a typical steam generation and distribution report for the mill of Fig. 8.2.

The daily steam-balance summary generally consists of data on total steam supplied to an individual header and total steam distributed from the header. The objective of a daily or hourly steam balance is the identification of any deviations from the established schedule. For example, the data in Table 8.2 indicate 4% unaccounted-for steam in the 885-psig header, 6% in the 385-psig header, and 3% in the 45-psig header. Utility engineers at most industrial plants feel that accounting for steam within 3% of the prescribed total is possible if the steam distribution system is not leaky and if the metering instruments are properly calibrated and maintained. A steam loss of more than 3% should be investigated and fixed.

The pressure-reducing valves (PRVs) between the steam-supply headers are important because they introduce irreversibilities and therefore add to the total energy cost. For example, Table 8.2 shows that 250,000 lb/day of steam was reduced by PRVs from 385 to 45

TABLE 8.2

Steam Balances for Pulp and Paper Mill Producing 1000 Tons of Pulp per Day[a]

Meter no.	Description	Steam (lb/day)
High-pressure header (885 psig)		
Supply		
100	Recovery BLR	10,000,000
102	Bark BLR	3,500,000
104	PWR BLR 1	3,680,000
106	PWR BLR 2	4,000,000
Distribution		
200	Soot blower	30,000
202	High-pressure BFW heater	50,000
204	BFW pump 1	470,000
206	TG 1	11,070,000
208	TG 2	9,560,000
210	PRV 1	0
	Unaccounted	840,000
Intermediate-pressure header (385 psig)		
Supply		
300	BFW pump 1	470,000
302	TG 1	7,370,000
304	TG 2	6,000,000
306	PRV 1	0
Distribution		
400	BFW pump 2	758,000
402	BFW pump 3	600,000
404	PRV 2	250,000
406	Process	11,402,000
	Unaccounted	830,000
Low-pressure header (45 psig)		
Supply		
500	BFW pump 2	758,000
502	BFW pump 3	600,000
504	PRV 2	250,000
506	TG 1	3,700,000
508	BLR BD drum	508,000
Distribution		
600	Deaerator	150,000
602	Process	5,401,000
604	Vent to atmosphere	100,000
	Unaccounted	165,000

[a] From Cho (1982).

psig. A close examination should be made to see whether there is an alternative allocation method that would provide the 45-psig steam without the use of a PRV.

There are different reasons for venting low-pressure steam. In general, steam venting is common during the summer, when the steam demand for heating is low but that for equipment and prime movers is high. Not every pulp mill or industrial plant has an excess-steam condenser. If such a condenser is present, the balance of low-pressure steam is maintained. The task of minimizing or eliminating the venting varies according to the many factors unique to each plant; some possibilities are selection of motor-driven prime movers, rather than steam turbines, evaluation of motor- and turbine-drive combinations, evaluation of the contract for purchase of power to make sure that the operation of motor-driven equipment is not in violation of the demand limit.

The energy management computer system has been extensively used to provide energy databases such as the one shown in Table 8.2. The plant snapshots of the energy balance for all the different utilities are also very useful tools for troubleshooting many potential problem areas.

C. Dedicated Microcomputer Applications

The low cost and accessibility of microcomputers have already had a far-reaching impact on the management-information industry. Their influence is often to be found in engineering applications because of the recent proliferation of microprocessor-based systems for real-time tasks in the process and manufacturing industry.

The so called user-friendly, high-level software with the capability for graphic displays to update process variables has attracted the attention of many engineers.

1. STEAM-BALANCE CALCULATIONS
   (Clary, 1983)

Computerized steam-balance programs can be used two ways. They can be used in a completely general method whereby the steam distribution system is described in terms of process units: headers, turbines, boilers, PRVs, etc. In such an arrangement they are connected to each other using a number of different flow-sheet arrangements. They can also model the system in which the process units are connected in one flow-sheet pattern only. The pattern selected should be as general as possible so that the majority of the systems that are subsequently modeled are simply subsets of the original system.

The advantages of the first approach are that the model is completely general and accuracies can be very good. However, it requires a great deal of computer memory; an iterative mathematical solution takes run times that are not insignificant.

The advantages of the second approach are that programming is fairly simple, run times are short, and memory requirements are small. However, the program only works for systems that can be modeled as a subset of the original system.

A utility complex having boilers, turbogenerators, process-condensing loads, condensate returns, a deaerator, a closed feedwater heater, and a boiler blowdown flash tank and heat recovery system (as well as some with fixed loads) can be modeled to simulate the plant steam and heat balance. This technique has helped design engineers to study and propose an optimum steam-balance diagram and associated equipment configurations for a new plant or plant-expansion project. To optimize energy allocation it helps to define new operating strategies for an existing steam distribution system.

A program of this nature has many applications, some of which are conceptual engineering studies that perform preliminary trade-offs with regard to system design and parametric studies that develop and predict performance at the various load levels of steam and electrical power, once the final design is selected.

A dedicated steam- and energy-balance system using a microprocessor-based system is a viable and economical way to continuously fine tune the distribution system to realize the maximum benefits of energy efficiency, in either an on-line or an off-line mode.

2. ON-LINE MONITORING AND DIAGNOSTICS
(Bannister *et al.*, 1983)

Today considerable effort is being directed to develop on-line monitoring and diagnostic systems that can be used for expensive plant equipment such as turbogenerators, compressors, refrigeration machines, and large fans. Microprocessor-based computer systems are widely used to detect a malfunction causing an alarm or trip with a broader information base for diagnostic tool and to advise operators of abnormal conditions before alarm levels are reached for troubleshooting.

Monitoring and diagnostic systems are intended to *complement* existing supervisory instrumentation systems not to replace them. Some recently completed or under development systems that may be adapted to an on-line surveillance system are the following.

(1) *Rotor Thermal Cycles and Cracks.* The heating and cooling of the turbine rotor during normal start-up and shutdown produces thermal stresses. Measurement of the actual rotor bore temperature is desirable to help minimize damage to rotor.

(2) *Water Induction.* In recent years the induction of water into large steam turbines has been a major cause of forced outages. An active ultrasonic system concept uses a pair of directive transmit–receive transducers that are coupled to the outside of a pipe. Water is detected by acoustic paths between transducers.

(3) *Steam Purity.* The presence of chloride and other impurities in steam can lead to stress-corrosion cracking or pitting of turbine parts. In the simplest diagnostic scheme, the influent and effluent for all chemically active components in the steam–water cycle is monitored for all chemicals of interest.

(4) *Generator Coolant Temperature.* Continuous monitoring of generator temperature is a proven method of protecting the generator against a complete failure.

(5) *Abnormal Arc Monitoring.* Long-term expensive outages that result from component failures such as starter-winding insulation failure, copper conductor fatigue failure, or voltage breakdown because of reduced clearances between components at different voltages can result from internal generator arcing. To monitor these currents, the radio-frequency currents developed by an arcing condition, a special high-frequency current transformer is connected around the generator's neutral grounding lead.

(6) *Vibration Analysis.* The evaluation of vibration response to

determine the dynamic health of operating equipment is an ongoing program. Today term-signature analysis or pattern recognition is applied to monitoring and analysis techniques that allow the operational dynamic health of a machine to be compared with baseline measurements to warn of equipment deterioration or potential damage.

The trend is to use microprocessors in a modular configuration in which each microprocessor handles specific tasks required by the entire system. The future turbogenerator control system may include a modular microprocessor approach to obtain higher reliability, decreased service time, and flexibility in application of control features to a particular unit.

9

Energy Management Opportunities in Selected Process Industries

This chapter highlights the unique opportunities for energy conservation in selected industries via improved process control and/or optimization. To a large extent, the opportunities for energy savings in different industries can be ascertained by examining their process operations, by-product fuels available for combustion processes, and the different sources of their energy supply.

Some of the major distinguishing elements of each industrial plant and its specific energy management opportunities are presented to give the reader some idea of the areas toward which effort may be directed to identify and quantify energy-savings opportunities.

The process industries can be generally grouped into the following categories (percentages indicate the energy consumed by the industry): chemical (25%), primary metals (29%), petroleum refining (17%), pulp and paper (14%), stone/clay/glass/concrete (8%), and food (7%).

The major energy users within the above-mentioned six industrial sectors are (percentages indicate fuel consumed by the unit operation) direct heating of process steams (39%), compression (7%), electrolysis (7%), evaporation (4%), drying (6%), cooking, sterilization, digestion (4%), feedstock (11%), and miscellaneous (22%).

The control strategies and optimization procedures presented in the previous chapters could be applied to the process industries, allowing for a certain amount of customization to fit the specific needs of the plant.

A. The Pulp and Paper Industry

The pulp and paper industry is one of the energy-intensive industries. Thus there has been a need for and a clear trend toward energy self-sufficiency through modernization of mills and their utility complexes.

However, differences between countries, mills, and end products determine the degree of a mill's dependency on purchased energy and its energy consumption. For example, a modern bleach-market pulp mill can be up to 90–100% energy self-sufficient. On the other hand, the energy self-sufficiency of a modern newsprint mill is only about 20%. As a whole, the energy self-sufficiency of the pulp and paper industry in the United States has increased from 41.5% in 1972 to 47% in 1978.

In the pulp and paper industry energy is mainly used in the form of steam, hot water, and electricity; most mills use turbines to generate mechanical-shaft horsepower for fans, compressors, and pumps. The primary fuels—natural gas, oil, and coal—are purchased for power boilers and lime kilns in kraft pulp mills. The steam is generated in recovery boilers, combination boilers (i.e., bark and the primary fuels), and power boilers. Some mills also purchase bark and wood residues to be used as fuels in the combination boilers.

The power boilers are mainly responsible for maintaining the set point of the high steam-distribution header pressure as swing boilers. Spent liquors in chemical and pulp mills are used as fuel in recovery boilers, and they provide a significant percentage of the total mill steam load.

Figure 9.1 shows a simplified flow diagram of chemicals and energy in a kraft mill. The major subsystems shown in Fig. 9.1—

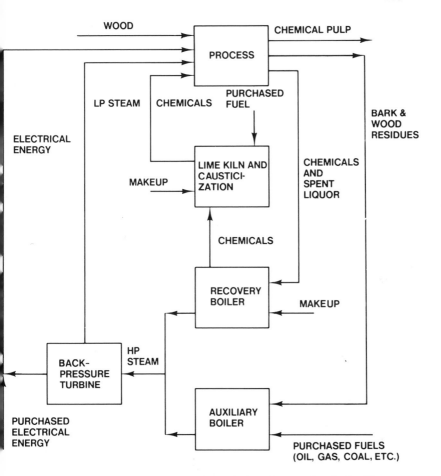

FIG. 9.1   Simplified flow diagram of chemicals and energy in a kraft mill.

process, lime kiln and causticization, recovery boilers, power boilers, and back-pressure turbines—are highly interactive in that mill production is closely related to these subsystems' ability to control and maintain target throughputs.

A simplified block diagram of overall energy balance for a kraft paper mill is shown in Fig. 9.2. In this case, high-pressure steam is supplied by auxiliary and recovery boilers. In addition to the purchased electricity and fuel shown in Fig. 9.2, low-pressure steam from turbines and by-product electrical power satisfy the energy demand imposed by various processes.

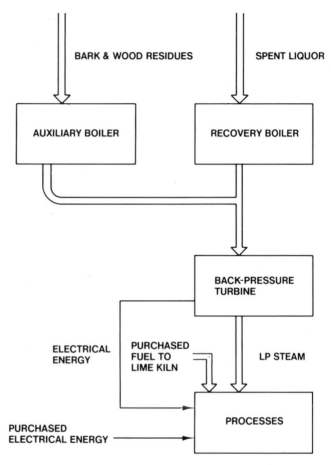

FIG. 9.2   Simplified block diagram of overall energy balance in a kraft paper mill.

The areas with the capacity for energy reduction can be grouped into the three major sectors: energy supply systems, energy distribution systems, and energy users. In general, energy management functions are evaluated beginning with the unit operations: control improvement and optimization. Then an overall coordinated strategy is developed to manage the entire complex in each of the three areas. Finally, a millwide energy management system is implemented as a high-level optimization procedure (Uronen, 1980).

1. ENERGY SUPPLY SYSTEMS

There are two major energy requirements in the paper industry: steam and electricity. These two utilities represent a significant portion of the total energy costs. Therefore, every mill manager looks for opportunities to reduce these energy costs.

Steam supply is usually met by recovery boilers (e.g., kraft pulp mills), bark, and power boilers. Normally, the recovery and bark boilers are base-loaded, and the power boilers are used as swing boilers to meet the mill's steam variations. The energy conservation strategy focuses on the maximum use of by-product fuels to minimize the use of primary fuels, e.g., oil, gas, and coal.

a. *Recovery Boiler (Fisher Controls*
   International, Inc., 1977)

Although the primary function of the recovery boiler is the recovery of chemicals for use in the batch digesters, the improved recovery-boiler steaming efficiency can contribute significantly to a reduction in purchased-fuel consumption.

The computer application of recovery-boiler control and optimization opportunities include many subsystems closely related to the chemical-reduction loop. These controls are recovery-boiler combustion, bed height, emission, production, evaporator, final liquid concentration, dissolving tank, and soot blowing.

Combustion, bed-height, emission, final liquid concentration, and soot-blowing controls have a direct impact on the steaming efficiency of the recovery boiler. Therefore, the ultimate average steam cost of a mill is closely influenced by the ability of these subsystems to maintain and control the optimum target set points.

The primary control function of the recovery boiler is recovery-boiler combustion control. This strategy should provide coordinated control of liquor, combustion, and excess air. Further boiler-control refinements should be attempted in the areas of smelt bed-height control, emissions control, and throughput optimization.

The multiple-effect evaporator control and final liquor-concentration control packages allow the final solids content of the liquor fired in the boiler to be maintained at a desired level. Maintaining precise solids content will contribute to stable boiler operation and high boiler efficiency.

The dissolving tank plays an important role in the recovery of the inorganic chemicals contained in the liquor burned in the recovery boiler. Dissolving-tank control should allow precise control of the dissolving-tank green-liquor total-titratable-alkali content. This will help to stabilize the recausticizing operation, reduce lime usage, and improve white-liquor quality.

Soot-blowing control provides automatic adjustment of spaced soot blowing to reflect boiler-solids throughput and operating conditions. Also, the soot blowing should be tailored to provide more frequent blowing in those areas that tend to plug up.

i. Combustion Control

Coordinated control of recovery-boiler combustion requires implementation of supervisory control in liquor flow and temperature and boiler air flows.

While on control, the solids throughput to the boiler are specified in gallons per minute of a standard liquor, a standard liquor being one with 62% solids content. Because the typical liquor-solids content is usually around 61–65%, the production rate should result in approximately the same change in liquor flow. Based on the heavy black–liquor-solids measurement, the liquor-flow set point is automatically changed to maintain the specified liquor-solids–throughput production rate. The liquor flow is changed at a controlled rate in response to a production-rate change.

Liquor and air flows into the boiler are continuously monitored and compared with a dynamic model of the combustion process. This model incorporates boiler measurements to continuously characterize the incoming black liquors. By decoupling excess boiler air from the consumed air (i.e., the air that takes part in combustion of the liquor), the model allows tighter control of total air flow and provides early detection and correction of blackout conditions.

The total boiler air flow is regulated to maintain the stack-oxygen set point. Adjustments to total air are limited to a maximum deviation from the air requirements projected by the consumed-air model. When the boiler production rate is changed, air and liquor flows are changed at a controlled rate to avoid upsetting the boiler operating conditions.

The boiler air distribution—split between the different air port levels—is calculated as a function of the boiler production rate. This air distribution can be trimmed based on SO_2 (sulfur dioxide) feedback.

While on control the final black–liquor-temperature set point can be precisely adjusted. Liquor temperature is trimmed based on the smelt–bed-height measurement if the bed-height option is purchased. In addition, when liquor and air flows are under automatic control, liquor temperature will be increased by a set amount if a blackout condition is detected.

ii. Bed-Height Control

With the addition of the bed-height control, liquor temperature is adjusted to maintain the bed height at an operator-specified set point. Actual smelt bed height is monitored through air-cooled television cameras located at two corners of the recovery boiler and displayed on dedicated television monitors located within the control console.

The control advantages gained by adding the bed-height option to recovery-boiler combustion control are more stable boiler operation by reduction in bed-height variation, more consistent and higher smelt reduction by maintaining proper bed height, and maintenance of correct liquor temperature, thereby minimizing dust carryover.

iii. Emissions Control

The boiler's air distribution, which is maintained by the basic recovery-boiler combustion control, is based on the boiler production rate. However, for a given production rate, the correct air distribution will vary slightly with liquor composition. Trimming of this air distribution from the calculated value to maintain chemical reduction at a high level, without creating excessive boiler dust loading, is the main feature of the emission control.

The manner in which dust loading varies with SO_2 emissions is established through tests. Instruments are available for the measurement of total reduced sulfur (TRS) and SO_2 emissions (on low-odor design boilers). Either of these measurements may be used to control dust emissions by trimming the primary air fraction determined by boiler–production-rate control. The deviation of the air distribution from the production-rate calculation is limited with either control approach. The selection of SO_2 emissions or TRS measurements for control of emissions depends on boiler design and user preference.

The control advantages gained by adding the emissions control option are the stabilization and possible reduction of liquor-system deadload because most of the boiler dust is collected at the ash hopper and/or precipitator and reinjected into the liquor system; the reduction of excessive dust loading, which can cause boiler pluggage, excessive soot blowing, and production time lost to boiler washout downtime; and the stabilization of and possible increase in smelt reduction.

iv. Production Optimization Control

Production optimization of the recovery boiler is designed to allow a recovery-limited mill to obtain the maximum recovery throughput. Using the basic recovery-boiler combustion control, the operator may set the production rate at a value that will keep the boiler operating close to the boiler's constraint. However, the tendency is for an operator to set the production rate low so that, without closely monitoring the constraint, he is assured that normal process variations will not cause the constraint to be exceeded. This margin is usually larger than necessary.

Production optimization allows numerous boiler constraints to be used to determine boiler–production-rate limits. These constraints must be detectable through process inputs (or calculations based on process inputs), known as constraining parameters, which are directly related to boiler production rate. Associated with each constraining parameter is a soft limit and a hard limit. The soft limit defines the point at which the production rate should not be increased to avoid exceeding the hard limit. The production rate is decreased at a controlled rate if the hard limit is exceeded. These parameters must be determined individually for each recovery boiler.

For a mill that is recovery limited, production optimization will allow the average recovery-boiler throughput to be increased. This increase is obtained by operating the boiler as close as safely possible to its operating constraints.

v. Final-Liquor Concentration

The solids content of heavy black liquor is an important parameter to boiler operations. Problems in the boiler such as plugged liquor guns result if heavy black-liquor solids are too high. Very low solids content is dangerous. Also, low levels of heavy black-liquor solids contribute to high SO_2 emission levels. Variations in heavy black-liquor solids effect other operational parameters such as energy input, liquor-droplet size, smelt-bed stability, are requirements, and steam generation.

The recovery–boiler-package control options available for the concentration of strong black liquor to heavy black liquor are concentrator, cascade, and cyclone controls. Coordinated optimum control of a concentrator requires implementation of control in concentrator steam and feed flows.

Concentrator steam flow is regulated to maintain the product solids at an operator-specified set point. Closed-loop control of product solids is based on a solids analysis provided by a continuous density analyzer. Steam pressure, temperature, and flow measurements are used to determine steam-mass flow to the concentrator. The steam-mass flow is regulated based on steam-chest pressure, inlet density, product density, and product-density set point. The chest pressure is used as an indicator of internal changes in the concentrator and is used in a unique manner in the steam-mass flow control. Feedforward control is provided when changes occur in concentrator feed and in product-solids set point.

Optimized control of concentrator feed allows throughput changes to be made at a rate that will not disrupt product solids. When the concentrator becomes steam limited (i.e., the steam valve is wide open), the concentrator throughput will automatically be reduced to allow steam-flow control to be maintained.

The major advantages of coordinated control over standard analog control of a concentrator are automatic regulation of the concentrator steam-mass flow to maintain product-solids content in spite of inlet-density changes, throughput changes, and concentrator fouling and reduction of variations in product solids to the liquor guns and maintenance of the product solids at the highest solids content determined by boiler and concentrator operating constraints.

vi. Soot-Blowing Optimization

The operation of a soot-blowing sequencer is the same regardless of boiler operating conditions. Like most boiler auxiliaries, the soot-blower system is designed to operate above the nominal-solids nameplate rating. When the boiler load is less than the maximum-solids firing capability of the unit, then continuous blowing should not be required. Thus, significant steam savings could be obtained by keying soot-blowing operation to boiler load. As load varies the soot-blowing cycle frequency can be varied. If a boiler is encountering pluggage, it is difficult to tailor a dedicated sequencer to provide more frequent blowing in the section that needs it most. This may force the boiler to be operated at less than maximum throughput or force more frequent shutdowns for boiler washdown.

The soot-blowing options provide automatic adjustment of spaced soot blowing to reflect boiler solids and operating conditions throughout the boiler. Also, the soot blowing can be tailored to provide more frequent blowing in those areas that tend to plug up.

The spacing used in soot blowing will be established according to the level of boiler solids. As boiler solids vary, soot-blower cycle frequency will be varied. Limited trimming of this basic function may be invoked through an engineer command. The rate of trimming action may be specified within a certain range. Adjustments should be made gradually, while key operating parameters are monitored for indications that more soot blowing is required. Once this point is established, the soot-blowing spacing should be decreased by a fixed safety margin, trimming action should be terminated, and a report printed that shows the before and after values of boiler efficiency, gas temperatures, and soot-blowing spacing.

Exit-gas temperatures from the boiler, economizer, and stack should be monitored. As a cleaning indicator, outlet temperatures should be kept in a band about the design value for these temperatures. In addition, steaming efficiency should be calculated by the heat-loss method, using off-line liquor analysis and measurements of the percentage of boiler solids.

The boiler will produce more pounds of steam per pound of solids if the boiler is clean. Thus monitoring steam efficiency will suggest when soot blowing must be increased or, conversely, when it may be decreased.

Boiler dust loading should be calculated based on the increase in liquor density after the precipitator and ash hopper have been used. Draft loss across the tube banks should be monitored. An increase in draft loss indicates a severe fouling problem. In the event of increased draft loss, continuous soot blowing should be immediately implemented and the operator notified of this condition.

Engineering functions for tailoring of soot blowing in each boiler section will be provided. Such adjustments allow a greater amount of soot blowing to be provided in the boiler section where pluggage occurs. The adjustments will be based on comprehensive inspections of the boiler surfaces made during boiler outage. This allows soot-blowing performance to be analyzed.

The operator should be able to revert back to his soot-blowing sequencer at any time. When on optimization control, the operator may request displays that, depending on hardware selected, give current control schedules and associated inputs and calculations.

The logic to determine which combinations of soot blowers to operate for a given condition, their priority, and the maximum time between successive operations of a specific soot blower is configurable from the engineer's keyboard to optimize the strategy according to individual boiler characteristics.

The hourly averages of all inputs associated with soot blowing, boiler efficiency, soot-blower spacing, and allocation of soot-blowing time to each boiler section should be stored for 30 days. This information may be trended or printed at the CRT or line printer. Such information will be used initially to determine soot-blower spacing and to monitor soot-blower performance.

The major advantages of implementing optimization control for soot blowing are reduced steam consumption caused by adjustment of spacing as a function of solids throughput and increased throughput caused by tailoring soot blowing to provide increased soot blowing where pluggage occurs.

b. Bark Boiler (Michaelson and Herrewig, 1983)

In many pulp mills and lumbering operations bark- or hog-fuel boilers burn wood wastes. These units provide steam from wood wastes that generally cost 4–6 times less than oil or gas at current prices.

Computer control of wood-fuel-fired boilers has been used in recent years to enhance the steaming efficiency of these boilers by better control and management of combustion processes associated with air breakthrough, excess-air control, and fuel-handling systems.

Wood–oil exchange control for a combined fired hog-fuel boiler utilizes a novel, multimode boiler master to maximize the use of the lowest cost fuel during combined firings. The computer application focuses on the implementation of hill-climbing techniques in concert with a model reference furnace-brightness routine in the wood–oil firing strategy using the multimode boiler master.

The objective of the multimode boiler master is to maximize low-cost fuel use during combined-fuel firing. It is a common practice to find hog-fuel boilers base-loaded and take their demand swings on a more consistent and easily fired fuel oil or gas. There are a number of reasons for this practice, including speed of response and ease of operation on oil, variation in the hog-fuel capacity of the boiler, mode of combustion (suspension versus bed firing), and inherent characteristics of the boilers with respect to their firing-rate constraints. In addition, the fuel can exhibit the following variable qualities: bulk density, composition, species, and moisture level.

With these constraints and fuel-property variables, operators are reluctant to fire wood fuel without oil support because the removal of the last oil gun would leave them in a poor position in the event of a bed blackout or a major load swing.

The system design philosophy includes

(1) efficiently utilizing the greatest possible percentage of hog fuel for each pound of steam produced, without causing operational problems,

(2) exchanging oil for wood during exhaust- or total–air-limited situations in which additional oil firing is necessary to meet the plant demand,

(3) meeting the demands of the plant by swinging on oil, oil and wood, or wood alone, depending on the fuel quality and the boiler load,

(4) allowing the operator to tune and shape the response of the control system based on his judgment of the hog-fuel quality and the observed response of the furnace,

(5) accommodating the daily grate-cleaning routine so that the operator may leave the controls in their normal operating mode.

A boiler master strategy that meets the above goals incorporates forced wood–oil exchange (hill climbing), exhaust constraints (ID fan speed), total air-supply constraints (FD fan speed), combustion constraints (relative brightness), a wood master with adaptive gains, an oil master with constraints and overrides, wood-feeder profiling and limiting, operator tuning of a hog "quality" control factor, and a grate-cleaning mode.

The wood–oil exchange uses a hill-climbing technique that continuously tries to increase the hog-fuel contribution to the total steam production. In a feedforward manner, it also removes the equivalent Btu value in oil until all of the oil guns have been removed, the minimum oil pressure has been reached, and the constraints associated with high ID fan speed and high FD fan amperes, low relative brightness, and high wood-feed limit have been reached.

The results of implementing this strategy have been an increased annual hog-fuel utilization of approximately 5%. Other improvements are apparent in increased boiler stability and combustion efficiency.

2. ENERGY DISTRIBUTION SYSTEMS
(Cho and Blevins, 1980)

There are often opportunities to exercise discretion in the use of generated steam in a plant. These opportunities may occur on short notice if process demand drops, or boiler capacity may be sufficient to routinely generate steam beyond process and space-heating requirements. Management of the steam network offers opportunities for savings by satisfying absolute as well as discretionary needs for heat and work in some optimal fashion.

Typical installations have boilers that generate steam at high pressure; this is expanded to several different pressure levels for use in the plant. The expansions may occur through units such as turbines or heat exchangers, in which case work or heat is extracted. The expansion may also occur through reducing valves, in which case all of the enthalpy is available at the lower pressure. Expansion policies can be established and enforced to ensure the most effective use of the available work and heat energy in the steam as it flows through the various headers. This requires that the state of the steam be known at the entrances and exits of all units and pressure-reduction stations and that calculations be performed to assign relative values to potentials for providing heat and work under given mill-operating conditions.

Turbogenerator management provides an opportunity for savings in operating expenses. By constraining the steam flows to satisfy both the process steam requirements and, through the turbogenerators, the kilowatt-hour demand requirements, the turbogenerator network will fulfill the needs of the process. On optimization, the cost of operation will be the lowest among the infinite combinations of process variables that satisfy the process requirements.

The steam distribution system is comprised of a number of steam headers ranging from high to low pressure. Steam balances are relatively straightforward calculations that show the material flows at the battery limits of the mills for given demands under various operating conditions.

The balances can be used to identify and investigate losses. If there are no leaks and metering instruments are properly calibrated and maintained, steam balances should be within 3% in each header. Venting is often the most easily corrected loss mechanism in pulp and paper mill steam distribution systems. Steam balances provide the data needed to establish operating policies that minimize venting.

Steam-accounting tasks include mass and energy balancing and Btu-usage monitoring for various process areas. Systems performing such accounting functions should, ideally, include the means to detect sudden or gradual deviations from previous operating values as indications of possible leaks, heat-exchanger fouling, or process problems. Historical data would also be useful for future planning.

3. DIGESTER CONTROL SYSTEM
(Fisher Controls International, Inc., 1977)

There are many opportunities for energy conservation in the pulp and paper process operations. In many instances, the process computer applications include energy savings as one of the important considerations for a computer application in process optimization.

Using a computer, the economics of batch-digester control systems for a pulp and paper mill can be justified based on liquid charging, reduced pulp-yield variability, steam smoothing, and throughput increase.

The steam smoothing function is selected to illustrate the type of energy conservation measures that can be incorporated as an integral part of the computer-based batch-digester control systems.

Steam is the key raw material in the production of pulp. Among batch-digester raw materials, steam is an anomaly in that its price can vary significantly, depending on the initial source: oil, gas, or bark. It is obviously more economical to heat digesters with more bark-generated steam than oil- or gas-generated steam.

Steam consumption can range from 4000 to over 6500 lb/ton of pulp. The amount of steam consumed per ton of pulp produced is dependent on the mill's products and operating philosophy, i.e., the cooking-time interval and temperature set points, gas-off procedures, initial heating with 50- to 60-psi steam, inclusion of blow-back steam, use of shake-down steam, and whether the units are directly steamed (no return condensate) or indirectly steamed (condensate available for pulp washing or feedwater depending on cleanliness). Shake-down steam refers to the direct injection of high-pressure steam into the cone area just prior to blowdown.

The initial liquor : wood ratio can also have a significant effect on the amount of steam required to reach and maintain the target cooking temperature. Wet woods require more steam heating to raise the temperature of the mass.

The kinetics of heat transfer prevent significant reductions in the average steam consumption per ton of pulp produced. That is, if the initial temperature of a digester's charge is 165°F and the target cooking temperature is 335°F, then a specific amount of saturated steam is required to elevate the temperature by 170°F.

Minor steam savings are available if the mill has loosely controlled or manual gas-off and blow-back operations. In these instances, the operator is inclined to gas-off too long, thus venting too much steam. The steam-consumption savings obtained from automatic control of gas-off and blow-back vary significantly from operation to operation. One can expect to save $20,000–$40,000/yr in steam consumption via gas-off and blow-back automation. More significant steam-related savings are available through steam-demand smoothing and digester scheduling.

Batch digesters consume steam on an intermittent basis. During the charging of chips and liquor to a directly steamed digester, no steam is applied. During the same operation to an indirectly steamed digester, some steam is applied to the liquor heater. During the steaming or ramping phase, a large amount of steam is continuously applied, regardless of direct or indirect design. Once the target cooking temperature is reached, the rate of steam application is greatly reduced to a level used only to maintain the desired temperature. Little or no steam is applied during the blow phase.

This sequence of consuming steam at a high rate, then a low rate, and then not at all places a heavy burden on the powerhouse to produce steam on demand and, just as suddenly, to reduce the steam-generating level when the capacity is not needed. The inefficiencies that result from swinging boiler loads to meet digester-house steam demands are also a large and unnecessary expense to the mill. Digital enforcement of digester-scheduling and steam-smoothing techniques can reduce steam-demand variations by 70 to 80%. Variations of ±35,000 to ±45,000 lb/hr of steam are common in a 10- to 15-unit batch house. The control system can reduce these swings to ±10,000 lb/hr or less by establishing and upper steam limit on the batch-digester house, scheduling the initiation of batch cooks to best use available steam, smoothing or distributing available steam among those digesters in the steaming phase, and shifting a greater percentage of the steam-generating load to the hog-fuel-fired boiler(s) from the more expensive, conventional oil- or gas-fired boiler(s).

An upper steam limit of, say, 140,000 lb/hr assures that the steam-consumption rate does not go above the limit. Thus, demands for more than 140,000 lb/hr are not satisfied. Instead, the steaming phase takes slightly longer to reach the target cooking temperature. This condition allows boiler operators to manage their units more efficiently to a stable output rate.

A 14-unit batch-digester house typically has four to six digesters in the steaming (ramp) phase at any one time. If four digesters are steaming, each is drawing 35,000 lb/hr of steam, and a fifth digester is brought on-line, then the steam demand is instantly increased by 25%. Scheduling, in concurrence with the desired production rate, stages the start-to-steam time to minimize excessive demands on the boiler house.

Steam smoothing takes over where digester scheduling stops. Smoothing reallocates the available steam among the digesters being steamed. For example, previously mentioned was the case where four units are drawing 35,000 lb/hr of steam and the upper limit is 140,000 lb/hr. When a fifth unit comes on-line, the control system proportionally reduces the steaming rate of the first four digesters to 28,000 lb/hr to accommodate the fifth unit and maintain the production rate. H-factor control ensures the proper blow time even with an erratic temperature profile. In this manner, swings in boiler efficiency and occasions of steam venting are greatly minimized.

With increased boiler stability resulting from limiting, scheduling, and smoothing control, one should shift 3–5% of the steam-generating load from the conventional-fuel boilers to hog-fuel boilers, thus realizing a substantial savings in purchased-fuel costs.

4. SUMMARY OF ENERGY-SAVING OPPORTUNITIES IN THE PULP AND PAPER INDUSTRIES

Many of the concepts, procedures, and optimization techniques described in Chapters 5–7 can be applied to paper mills. It is important to recognize that, in each selected application, a certain customization is required for system implementation. The list of potential applications and energy-savings opportunities are the following:

(1) upgrading of boiler instrumentation for combustion efficiency improvements in bark, hog-fuel, combination, recovery, and power boilers,
(2) optimum allocation of boiler fuels,
(3) steam-load allocation among the swing boilers based on real-time unit costs,
(4) steam distribution optimization and turbogenerator management,
(5) power-demand control and tie-line control and optimization,
(6) mill water management system for recycling reusable water,
(7) batch-digester control and steam smoothing,
(8) energy accounting system,
(9) application of linear programming technique for millwide utility optimization, and
(10) other unit operations.

B. The Steel Industry

The steel industry uses about 5% of the total energy consumed in the United States, or 17% of the total energy used by all industry.

On the basis of average Btu consumption per raw steel ton, coal supplies two-thirds of the process energy needs, with the remainder being provided by natural gas, oil, and purchased electricity. Furthermore, the usage is concentrated in relatively few large, integrated plants that are, individually, major energy users (Cho, 1981).

Many modern steel plants use computer control and the same process computers used for steel plant automation work well with energy management systems. The computer functions in energy management generally involve data acquisition and display, log and alarms, and performance calculation of utility systems (e.g., boilers, turbogenerators and compressors), and control optimization. Many computer manufacturers offer application technology and software for energy system optimization.

Management information systems can be designed to give the utility operating personnel real-time information and historical data on the steel mill operations. The information can be used to develop a better operating philosophy and future energy planning.

1. UTILIZATION OF BY-PRODUCT FUELS

Industry data indicate that steel manufacturing uses 22–25 MBtu per raw steel ton, of which about 69% is from coal, 18% from natural gas, 9% from oil, and 4% from purchased power. Therefore, purchased-fuel costs constitute a large portion of a plant's total energy cost. The optimum utilization of by-product fuels in the powerhouse and processes is the single most important function that can lead to a substantial reduction in expensive purchased-fuel costs.

The objective of a fuel management system is the provision of sufficient real-time information concerning the availability and consumption of both by-product gases and purchased fuel, so that the fuel-dispatch personnel can maximize the use of by-product fuels.

It is reasonable to assume that there may be as many as five different fuels used in a system. It is important to have accurate data on these fuels before an optimum fuel-dispatch policy can be implemented in an integrated steel plant. By-product fuels include coke-oven gas [500 Btu/scf (avg)], blast-furnace gas [90 Btu/std. ft^3 (avg)], and coal tar [160,000 Btu/gal (avg)]. Purchased fuels are natural gas [1100 Btu/std. ft^3 (avg)] and No. 6 oil [170,000 Btu/gal (avg)].

TABLE 9.1
Energy Suppliers' and Users' Matrix[a]

Fuel type

Process	Coal		Oil		NG		Coal	Tar	COG		BFG		Mixed gas		kW·h		Steam	
	U	S	U	S	U	S	U	S	U	S	U	S	U	S	U	S	U	S
Coke	×							×										
Blast furnace			×				×		×			×						
Blast-furnace stoves					×						×							
Boilers	×		×		×								×					
Basic oxygen furnace					×													
Open hearth			×		×													
Electric furnace															×			
Reheat furnaces			×		×								×					
Soaking pits			×										×					
Waste-heat boilers																		
Space heaters					×								×					
Boilers			×								×		×					×
Turbogenerators																×	×	

[a] U = users, S = suppliers, mixed gas = coke-oven gas (COG) + natural gas (NG) + air. From Cho (1981).

The goal of the fuel-dispatch system is to monitor, log–store, and display the firm- and swing-fuel users throughout the plant so that operating personnel have complete access to the respective flow rates, accumulated totals, and fuel types. This information can be arranged and displayed in the format most useful to the specific plant for an economic fuel dispatch (see Table 9.1.)

As the coke-oven gas (COG) and blast-furnace gas (BFG) come off the process unit, they must be managed and distributed to their users via distribution headers while minimizing, venting, or flaring. Coke-oven gas is pressure-sensitive; holding a pressure set point of, for example, 5 psig in its distribution header requires a good control system with the ability to maintain the supply pressure.

Blast-furnace gas is also pressure sensitive because of the large demand fluctuations imposed by its users: boilers, blast-furnace stoves, etc. The by-product gas distribution system should include on-line, automatic allocation of fuels based on availability, predetermined priority, and user requirements. For example, blast-furnace gas could be substituted for coke-oven gas for as long as it is available, thus delaying the switch to auxiliary fuels such as natural gas and/or oil.

The key to effective fuel management using a computer-based data acquisition system is the ability to present the data in the manner and format with which a logical fuel-dispatching decision can be made. Obviously, the specifics of data display, format, and historical log must be decided by the system's users to that the software can be accordingly developed for this purpose. The following reports have been identified as beneficial for an economic fuel-dispatching program.

a. *Daily Reports*

Daily fuel-consumption production-unit reports are from midnight to midnight by fuel type and percentage of Btu for each fuel type. An example of such a report is shown in the accompanying tabulation. Thus fuel consumption for the production unit equals the grand total of Btu's per ton.

Fuel type	Btu total	Btu %
Natural gas (XXX Btu/std. ft³)		
Quantity = XXX std. ft³	XXX	XXX
Coke-oven gas (XXX Btu/std. ft³)		
Quantity = XXX std. ft³	XXX	XXX
Blast-furnace gas (XXX Btu/std. ft³)		
Quantity = XXX std. ft³	XXX	XXX
No. 6 oil (XXX Btu/gal)		
Quantity = XXX gal	XXX	XXX
Total	XXX	

The plant's total daily consumption report is from midnight to midnight by fuel type. An example is shown in the accompanying tabulation.

Fuel type	Total quantity
COG	XXX std. ft³
BFG	XXX std. ft³
NG	XXX std. ft³
Coal tar	XXX gal
No. 6 oil	XXX gal

The plant's total daily purchased natural gas consumption report is for a gas day (8 a.m. to 8 a.m.).

b. *4-Day Demand Log*

Log and maintain a 4-day history by hour for each fuel type by area.

c. *35-Day Demand Log*

Log and maintain a 35-day history by day for each fuel type by area.

d. *Swing Users*

On a demand basis, all the swing users and each user's fuel type should be displayed on a CRT, including the individual consumption rates.

e. *Blast-Furnace Gas (BFG) Production*

With the metered information on blast-furnace fuel consumption (coke, No. 6 oil, and coal tar), the following calculation can be performed to estimate total BFG production, which allows the gas dispatcher to run a BFG balance of the plant:

$$\text{total BFG} = [\text{total air supply to furnace}][f(\text{coke, tar, oil})]$$

f. *Coke-Oven Gas Production*

With a manual entry of the total tons of coal charged to batteries, the following calculation can be made to account for the total COG production:

$$\text{COG produced/day} = \text{tons of coal} \times XXX \text{ ft}^3/\text{ton}.$$

This information can be used to develop a COG balance.

Whereas steel plant facilities are generally designed with alternative fuel capabilities, certain steel processing applications such as soaking pits, reheating furnaces, annealing, heat treating, and coating lines have no practical alternative using oil and gas fuels. Further, many plants have taken advantage of the benefits of natural gas or oil to increase production of such units as blast furnaces, open hearths, and basic oxygen furnaces. To reduce the consumption of expensive fuels, the possibility of interchanging by-product fuels and auxiliary fuels in many applications is being investigated by the steel industry.

2. ENERGY MODEL (Gray *et al.*, 1974)

Energy models have been used in steel plants to develop the utilities' dispatch policies: economic fuel dispatch, optimum plant-load allocation, and scheduling of equipment maintenance and shutdown. The model is designed to solve the problem of instantaneous steam and electrical power demands on a real-time basis or to operate on an off-line simulation mode, giving "how-to" solutions for minimizing the plant's energy costs. The most commonly used optimization technique is a linear programming method that uses a plant model.

The model is structured as a linear objective function with system constraints, e.g., physical limitations on utilities production, demands for utilities, and contractual limitations. The objective function equals the total cost of plant energy, taking into consideration purchased fuels and power and any other utility cost.

a. *Developing the Model*

To develop a linear programming model of the plant energy system, energy flows in the form of material and energy balances in each area of the utility system should be described using linear relationships, i.e., equations and inequalities.

Each relationship contains decision variables that represent a quantity of a given form of energy being used for a specific purpose (e.g., fuel required per ton of production, steam required per megawatt-hour generated, and steam-distribution header balances).

b. *Data Gathering*

The initial task in the development of a model is the gathering of information on the types and quantities of fuel that could be used by each facility and the determination of values for all the parameters. A summary sheet of a shift, daily, weekly, and monthly log on utility operations is a good source from which these data can be obtained. The source of information can be shown as

(1) historical data including energy usage per ton kept by the power and fuels department for areas such as soaking pits, reheating furnaces, and continuous-process lines,

(2) discussions with operating personnel, particularly in connection with mill practice restrictions and physical capacities (For use in the model, the capacity of a unit must reflect its average capacity over a period of time rather than its peak operating capacity.),

(3) theoretical relationships, in which insufficient historical data exist (e.g., theoretical combustion calculations can be used to determine the relationship of blast temperature and wind volume to the quantity of blast-furnace gas required for heating the blast-furnace stoves), and

(4) regression analysis for developing the relationship between electric power usage and production.

c. *Major Areas of the Plant Model*

i. Coke Plants

The amounts of medium- and high-volatile coal charged into the coke ovens are treated as input loads. The following parameters are generally considered in the model of coke ovens: coal-to-coke yield, coke-oven gas produced per ton of coal charged, coke-oven gas consumed for underfiring per ton of coal charged, and tar produced per ton of coal charged. The material and energy balance of mixed gas equals coke-oven gas plus natural gas injected into the mixed-gas system.

ii. Blast Furnaces

Input loads for the blast furnaces include hot-metal production, coke, oil, tar, wind, oxygen, and blast temperatures. A blast-furnace model can be built with the metered and measured input loads. However, there are some difficult measurement problems associated with the inputs and the blast-furnace gas flows. For this case, it may be necessary to rely on the experience of the operating personnel to estimate the values.

iii. Powerhouse

Blast-furnace gas is generally used in the powerhouse as a boiler fuel. The blast furnace uses the steam from the powerhouse to generate wind for the blast furnaces. Boiler models are usually obtained by the boiler characterization test to determine the operating characteristics of the boiler (efficiency versus boiler load). Turbogenerator models can be built using manufacturer's performance maps with the electrical power as a function of the throttled steam.

iv. Steel-Making Shops

Fuel requirements in steel-making shops are related to hot-metal practice, that is, the percentage of hot metal and scrap that make up the charge. Since there are only a limited number of practices, the tons produced at each practice are treated as input loads and the fuel requirements per ton for each practice are parameters based on historical data. The mix of oil and gas to satisfy the fuel needs is based on steel-making practice and is not subject to alteration by the model.

The open-hearth shops utilize waste heat to produce steam that is then available to the plant steam system. This is included in the model using parameters based on historical data.

v. Soaking Pits and Reheating Furnaces

A soaking pit or reheating furnace model is based on the type of fuels it is using. They use their own operating constraints and a set of fuel types that they can utilize. The Btu per ton requirements are obtained from the historical data.

d. *Operation*

There are basically three different computer programs: the matrix generator, the linear programming routine, and the report writer. A matrix generator converts the mill models into the format required by the linear programming routine. The linear programming routine is a computer program that optimizes the linear combination of energy costs subject to a set of linear constraints. The report writer summarizes the linear programming output and displays the decision variables in a useful format including the total mill energy operating cost.

The plant model should be verified using snapshots of the mill's operating conditions. These should be checked against the predicted total consumption of each fuel. Once the model is properly calibrated and verified, it is ready to be put into operation.

In addition to the model's use in daily utility management systems, it also offers a number of other off-line simulation opportunities such as the evaluation of various facilities' options for meeting plant steam and power requirements and the assistance in long-range facility planning of future expansion or replacement of old equipment.

3. SUMMARY OF ENERGY-SAVING OPPORTUNITIES IN THE STEEL INDUSTRY

Many of the recommendations enumerated in the previous section concerning the paper industry will work well in steel mills. The following list is offered as a general guideline for the energy-saving opportunities in steel mills:

(1) instrumentation upgrading and application of advanced control for boilers, furnaces, and unit operations including modification for flexibility of swing-fuel firing,

(2) by-product fuel management to maximize use of coke-oven gas, coal tar, and blast-furnace gas through an optimum fuel-dispatch system, including by-product gas header control,

(3) steam allocation among the swing boilers based on real-time unit costs,

(4) steam distribution optimization and turbogenerator management,

(5) power-demand control and tie-line control and optimization,

(6) optimization of unit operations, e.g., using models,

(7) application of linear programming technique for millwide utility optimization, and

(8) energy accounting system.

C. The Refining Industry (Gorindan, 1982)

Similar to other industries, the refining industry has taken a phased approach when undertaking energy management projects. They began by improving housekeeping and operating facilities, then continued by making modifications in existing equipment, making major changes requiring capital investment in new equipment and improved control, making major process changes in existing plants, and using new technologies that are less energy intensive (Edgar, 1980).

1. MODIFICATION IN EXISTING EQUIPMENT

During the early 1970s, major efforts were directed toward the improvement of combustion efficiency in boilers and fired heaters through better monitoring and control. Many of the problems associated with the boiler equipment such as burners, fuel-handling systems, and air-delivery systems have been alleviated through the use of better-maintained or modified equipment to improve the boiler and heater combustion efficiency. The automatic stack-gas control system with O_2 or CO stack-gas measurement has been widely used in many plants. In addition to the many other tasks they handle, computers have been widely used in recent years to optimize low excess firing.

2. NEW EQUIPMENT AND IMPROVED CONTROL

Waste-heat recovery can contribute to substantial energy savings in refining and petrochemical plants. However, these projects warrant a detailed engineering analysis and evaluation of costs and benefits.

In general, the heat-recovery operation should satisfy the conditions in which there are a supplier and a user in close proximity so that the recovery operation will not incur a high expense for piping and insulation.

An important consideration for the maintenance of a good heat balance in a plant is the choice of a steam turbine or an electrical

TABLE 9.2
Mechanical Energy Costs Based on Different Sources[a]

Driver	Cost ($/hp·yr)
Electric motor	205
Back-pressure turbine	145
Condensing turbine: 600-psig, 750°F throttle to 4-in. Hg A condenser	540
Condensing turbine: 30-psig throttle to 4-in. Hg A condenser	1060
Small turbine exhausting to atmosphere: 600-psig, 750°F throttle to atmosphere	2000

[a] Based on $5/MBtu for fuel, $0.03/kW·h for electricity, and a steam system operated at 600 psig, 715°F, 1 yr = 8500 hr.

motor to provide mechanical energy. Table 9.2 shows the order of magnitude of mechanical-energy costs based on different sources of energy and modes of operation. Selection of new equipment, e.g., steam turbines, electrical drives, and combination (dual drives: steam turbine or electrical motor), requires a careful analysis of the plant's steam-balance and heat requirements using historical data.

Many energy management computer systems are configured to generate the type of information given in Table 9.2 during the first phase of system implementation as a part of data acquisition and calculation functions. This real-time information is used to realize minimum energy operating costs by further defining and enforcing the optimum steam distribution and energy allocation policy. Obviously, these functions can be designed to be a part of the linear programming solutions if it is warranted.

3. PROCESS CONTROL

Process control involves computer control of fractionation towers to optimize reflux ratio and number of trays; integration of distillation trains, heat-pump optimization, feed preheat, and side draw-off; and reduction of valuable product loss. The control strategies generally take into account the relative importance of maintaining overhead purities, bottom purities, flow rates, and boil-up rates. At present there is great interest in evaluating the use of advanced control techniques, such as multivariable control, for distillation.

In the distillation processes, multivariable control can contribute to minimum energy costs by operating closer to the desired product set points and by increasing the recovery of desired product. The models used to design these controllers are generally more exact and account for multivariable interactions. Therefore, the distillation process can be carried out with minimum set-point variations.

Modifications on interreboilers and intercondensers can provide significant reductions in fuel consumption and distillation tower costs. The chief advantage of these devices lies in the ability of the system to utilize different levels of heat, some of which may be closer to ambient temperature. In addition, the possibility of flooding in a column is alleviated because of reduced liquid and vapor loading below an interreboiler and above an intercondenser.

A heat pump transfers energy from the condenser and uses work to raise the energy level of the working fluid high enough that it can be used in the reboiler. The implementation of a heat pump *does* reduce energy requirements for most columns, but this reduction must be weighed against increased capital costs and an increase in operational complexity. Matching of heating and cooling loads using the heat pump will usually not occur, thus necessitating the use of trim reboilers and condensers or some form of energy storage.

The heat pump can be installed with an independent working fluid, but normally the tower overhead stream can be compressed to yield a high enough temperature for heat addition to the reboiler (referred to as an open heat pump or vapor recompression). The economics of this plan depend largely on the pressure difference required by the compression step.

One other variation of the heat-pump principle is the split column, in which one column is operated at a high enough pressure that the overhead can be used for a heat source in the reboiler of the second column. In either of the above cases, the control difficulties created by the process-design changes could be significant; no detailed study of this problem has appeared in the available literature.

A common unit-operation sequence in refining and chemical plants requires the use of a series of distillation columns to obtain a set of products of desired purity, e.g., the overhead product of the first column is used to provide reboiler heat in the second column.

4. SUMMARY OF ENERGY-SAVINGS OPPORTUNITIES IN THE REFINING INDUSTRY

In the refining industry the opportunities for energy savings in the utility complex are similar to those in all industries; the only difference lies in the operating constraints and energy sources of both purchased and by-product fuels. These savings opportunities include instrumentation upgrading and the application of advanced control for boilers, fired heaters, and heat recovery systems; maximized use of by-product gases; steam allocation among swing boilers based on real-time unit costs; steam distribution optimization, taking into consideration the steam sources and users on the individual steam distribution header bases; turbogenerator management, power-demand control, and tie-line control; energy accounting systems; and advanced process-control and heat-recovery operations.

D. The Chemical Industry

The chemical industry has such diverse characteristics associated with each plant that it is difficult to generalize the energy-saving opportunities. Reactors are probably the most profit-sensitive elements of the plant, yet they are the most complicated and the least likely to be replicated from one plant to the next (Edgar, 1980).

In addition to the utility management opportunities that are summarized for each of the previously described industry types, some of the energy conservation approaches unique to the following chemical processes are presented briefly. When producing chlorine-alkali, energy may be conserved by lowering electrolytic voltages and current density, using triple-effect evaporators, using by-product hydrogen for boiler fuel, and providing steam and electrical power by cogeneration. Energy may be conserved when producing industrial gases by the recovery and use of waste heat, by process integration, and by the reduction of compression losses.

The production of pigments and paints can achieve energy conservation by the recovery and use of waste heat and low-heating-value fuel, improved drying efficiency, and the replacement of steam ejectors. One may save energy when producing plastics by the reduction of separation-energy requirements and the recovery and use of waste heat.

Pharmaceutical producers may reduce energy use by the use of by-product gases and the recovery and use of waste heat.

When producing coal-tar chemicals, energy may be conserved by the recovery and use of waste heat and off-gases, heat exchanger cascading, and improved energy efficiency in drying and distillation.

Agricultural-chemical production can reduce energy consumption by the recovery and use of waste heat and improved plant scheduling, shutdown, and start-up. Producers of ethylene can conserve energy by the recovery and use of waste heat, better utilization of low-pressure steam, optimization of refrigeration systems, and more intercooling in compression.

E. The Textile Industry

The textiles industry is the tenth most energy-intensive process industry in the United States. Energy sources for the industry generally include natural gas, coal, oil, and electric power, either purchased and/or cogenerated (Stecco *et al.,* 1981).

There has been concerted effort in the textiles industry, as in other industries, to develop an energy accounting system that would identify and quantify the energy-consumption standard. The energy management computer system is widely used, and one of its functions is the development of the database for the energy per unit production for each of the processes in the production areas or cost centers.

The processes involved in the production of textiles can be grouped into two categories: the dry process for the formation of yarn and fabric and the wet process for dying and finishing. Energy conservation opportunities for both of these processes exist largely in the utilities: steam, electrical power, chilled water, and water in the wet-end processes. Some of the energy management potentials for the textiles industry are summarized as follows.

Steam energy may be conserved by

(1) boiler efficiency improvement through upgrading of instrumentation, automatic excess-air trim, and advanced control;

(2) optimum allocation of boiler load;
(3) scheduling of boiler maintenance based on real-time information on boiler performance;
(4) economic dispatch of fuels conforming to the operating and resources constraints;
(5) improvement of condensate recovery through automation of the condensate-quality monitoring; and
(6) steam header-pressure control to prevent steam venting and minimize PRV flows.

Conservation of electrical power energy may be achieved by

(1) power-demand control;
(2) tie-line control in concert with optimum cogeneration policy, e.g., make or buy decisions, or instances in which one can sell electrical power to the local utility company or the plants in the vicinity; and
(3) turbogenerator optimization, e.g., kilowatt load allocation taking advantage of steam-path efficiencies or condensing-generation costs between the turbogenerators.

Chilled-water management systems can conserve energy by

(1) chiller-performance monitoring for scheduling maintenance and troubleshooting, where the chiller model in horsepower per ton versus load can be developed for these purposes;
(2) chiller-load allocation based on unit operating costs; and
(3) optimization including chiller energy, chilled- and condensing-water pumping, and auxiliary equipment costs.

Unit operations can conserve energy through the use of

(1) heat exchangers to regenerate waste water from dye baths;
(2) drying operations to recover heat in the dryer air, thus minimizing overdrying; and
(3) wastewater utilization, e.g., multistage evaporation, multistage flash distillation, or vapor-compression distillation.

F. The Total-Energy Plant

The concept of a total-energy plant has been receiving considerable attention recently among industrial plants and institutions. The total-energy plant offers good economic incentives for the users of steam, electricity, and chilled water for process cooling and air conditioning.

A total-energy plant can be privately owned by an institution or can be a cooperative venture in which a number of industrial plants or institutions in close geographical proximity share the utilities.

Medical Area Service Corporation (MASCO) operates a total-energy plant providing utility services for the ten hospital and research facilities in Boston that are affiliated with Harvard University. Boston's medical-area total-energy plant is a good example of the total-energy-plant concept. Since its inception MASCO has changed its name to Cogeneration Management Inc. (CMI), which operates the utility complex. The material contained in this chapter is based on CMI's (formerly MASCO) case history.

MASCO served as a planning organization for the first phase of the proposed total-energy plant, and the following factors were carefully evaluated: replacement of obsolete steam generators and of chilled-water plants with more efficient chillers, on-site generation of electricity, and environmental impact of a total-energy plant located in the midst of a thriving metropolis.

MASCO's main objectives for a total-energy plant were the reduction of high electricity costs in the area and the satisfaction of the large round-the-clock energy-consumption requirements of the member hospitals. Through cogeneration of steam and electricity it targeted a far lower overall plant heat rate and installed cost per kilowatt than a conventional plant.

Utilities to be provided included 51.9-MW electrical power, 994,000-lb/hr steam, 21,900 tons refrigeration, 42,840-gpm cooling water, and 1,150,000-gal oil storage.

Equipment selected for the utility complex included three 650-psi primary steam generators, two heat-recovery steam generators (i.e., those using heat from diesel engine exhaust), six diesel generators, two extracting–condensing turbogenerators, and two steam–turbine-driven and three electrical–motor-driven chillers.

1. OPERATING PHILOSOPHY

The plant's operating objectives are to reliably meet instantaneous customer demands while providing adequate spinning and steaming reserves and minimizing fuel costs. A combination of electronic analog controls and operator assistance from a digital computer will be used. The analog systems will provide combustion control for conventional boilers and diesel exhaust incinerators, frequency control of diesel engine generators, steam pressure control of PRV stations and extracting–condensing turbine generators, etc. The computer acquires and displays plant operating data, predicts load levels, and selects appropriate combinations of equipment to be operated. Plant operating economy will be further enhanced by utilization of the computer for plant data-logging functions including the preparation of plant-emissions reports.

Although the primary production equipment has good thermal efficiency, there would be little advantage to a total-energy plant if it were not for the auxiliary production equipment: the heat-recovery steam generators (HRSGs) and extracting–condensing steam-turbine generators (STGs).

The HRSGs perform two major functions. First, they incinerate the diesel engine exhaust by raising the temperature to 1500 to 1800°F for removal of unburned particulate matter from the exhaust, thus controlling particulate emissions from the engines to satisfy air pollution regulations. This allows the use of No. 6 oil as a diesel fuel. Then, the hot gas is used to generate steam, thus recovering most of the available heat from both the diesel exhaust and the No. 2 oil used for incineration.

The STGs also serve multiple functions. First, when the user's steam requirements are met with extraction steam, the units are very efficient sources of electricity. Second, operating in the condensing mode, the STGs provide the necessary sink for excess steam generated by the HRSGs in the summer. Finally, the STGs are equipped with speed governors that enable them to provide part of the electrical system spinning reserve.

Because most of these loads are services to either hospitals or research facilities, they must have a high degree of reliability. The service must be at least as reliable as if it were obtained from the local public utility. Thus, spin and steam reserve capacity must be adequate to cover a forced outage of any electrical generator or boiler. The plant is expected to carry the system loads and refrigeration requirements with an overall thermal efficiency of 60 to 80%. The higher efficiencies will occur in the winter when there is high demand for extraction steam. The lower efficiencies will occur in the summer when it will be necessary to condense part of the steam produced. The high plant efficiency is based on the high efficiency of diesel engines plus the effect of producing electricity from extraction steam, thus avoiding condenser heat loss.

2. CONTROL PHILOSOPHY

The control system utilizes a combination of local and central control. Local control panels at each piece of equipment provide for full manual control of the equipment. Major pieces of equipment are started from these panels, then the control normally transfers to the central control room after the unit is either on-line or ready to go on-line. Sufficient controls are available at the local panels so that the entire plant can be operated under manual control in the event the control room is not available.

The central mechanical-systems control panel contains controls and instrumentation for fuel-oil storage, pumping, and heating, steam-generator operation, feedwater and condensate, steam-system operation, vibration and trend recorders, chilled-water pumping and flow, cooling-water system operation, weather indication, and plant and tunnel conditions.

The design objective for this panel is the provision of a reasonably detailed visual indication of plant status and the provision of sufficient controls for normal operation. The operator is also able to take emergency action in response to system malfunction alarms.

a. *Electrical Power Generation*

Control of electric power generation is based on the speed-control capability of the diesel engine–generator governors. Electricity production of the STGs is normally determined by steam-system requirements. However, the units do have speed governors, which provide droop speed control. Thus the plant operator may simultaneously increase unit load and have the units automatically back up the engine generators by increasing output as system frequency drops.

b. *Diesel Incinerator Control System*

Incineration of exhaust gases from diesel engines burning heavy fuel is required to meet air pollution regulations for particulate emissions. This incineration takes place in HRSGs in which the furnace temperature is controlled at 1500 to 1800°F.

c. *Station and Boiler Master Controls*

The station's master combustion-control signal is derived from the 650-psi steam-header sections. The controller output is split between the boiler masters and the turbine-generator speed governors. Thus the boilers are fired to control steam-header pressure, but if firing is at a minimum and pressure continues to rise, the turbine speed governors will cause the turbines to take more steam, which causes increased generator output. The boiler master controls are biasing-type auto–manual stations that provide the output-control signal for the individual steam generators.

d. *Chiller-Load Control*

The chilled-water distribution system is operated on a constant temperature basis, e.g., 40°F leaving the plant and 55°F returning. The 40°F leaving temperature is controlled by individual chiller compressor controls.

e. *Fuel-Header Control*

Fuel-header pressure is controlled by back-pressure control recirculation valves. This system, in combination with the pump sets, maintains adequate pressure on the feeds to the boilers and the diesel engine fuel modules.

f. *Cooling-Tower Control*

Plant design provides for two symmetrical banks of four cooling-tower cells each. Each bank has identical controls that change cell fan speed and open a tower bypass valve as is necessary to maintain tower discharge temperature within preset limits.

3. COMPUTER SYSTEM

Because of the complexity of plant operation, a computer system is provided to continuously scan prescribed inputs, alarm off-normal values, and store, manipulate, display, and print them in various ways to generally inform, assist, and make the plant personnel more effective in the performance of their duties.

The computer software package provides all the usual process computer functions such as input scanning, alarming, printing, logging, and various summary displays and single-point operations. It has the added flexibility that the computer operator defines and can modify all input definitions, alarms, displays, logs, trend recordings, and historical databases. These will be entered at plant start-up time by a conversational interchange with the computer and can be modified with the computer on-line.

The computer has as inputs all analog signals being displayed or recorded in the control room, all information required for major equipment operating logs, direct temperature signals such as diesel-cylinder temperatures, all control-room annunciator operations, major equipment status contacts, and customer steam flow and pressure, condensate flow, chilled-water flow and temperature, and electricity usage.

The computer provides up to 150 accumulations of the following types: analog input, pulse counting, absolute value of the difference of two inputs, and discrete input time on. The system stores the following totals for each accumulation index: 24 hourly totals, 3 shift totals, 31 daily totals, and 12 monthly totals. These totals are accessible for CRT display, printing, or manipulation. Approximately 50 will be used for electrical, steam, and chilled-water utility-usage record keeping.

Historical database storage capability is provided for 64 points at 1-min intervals for 24 hr and for an additional 128 points at hourly intervals for 2 months. The data may be played back in tabular form or plotted and the hourly interval data may be transmitted through a 9-bit serial interface to a management information system (MIS) computer for storage and analysis. The MIS computer is well suited for voluminous data storage and complex analysis, whereas the plant computer is not. This hourly data is expected to be user-usage data to assist the customers in energy management. The 1-min interval data review can be useful for analysis of plant equipment or systems.

All of this data is available to the control-room operator as single-point or group CRT displays or printouts. The following computer outputs are of particular significance:

(1) the alarm printer output, which automatically records all an-nunciator operations, all computer-generated alarms and clears, and all equipment status changes and thus provides a chronological history of plant events,

(2) major equipment daily or shift log sheets,

(3) customer utility-service bills.

(4) up to nine analog outputs of any variables in the database to drive trend-recorder pens.

The computer is specially programmed to help the operator sched-ule equipment on- and off-line. To do this, the computer will have the following inputs available:

(1) table of the availability of steam generators, electricity gener-ators, and chillers with appropriate minimum-load, normal maximum-load, and emergency maximum-load data, all as entered into the computer by the operator;

(2) analog signals of current output and fuel or electricity input of each piece of major production equipment;

(3) analog signals of plant output to the distribution system of steam, electricity, and chilled water;

(4) analog signals of outdoor dry-bulb and wet-bulb temperature and wind speed and direction; and

(5) internal time and date.

The computer utilizes these inputs and provides the following outputs:

(1) an hourly printout of 1-, 2-, 3-, and 4-hr forecasts of system steam, electricity, and chilled-water demands,

(2) a listing of equipment that should be operated to meet each of the forecast loads with adequate spinning and steaming re-serves, with mode of operation of the HRSGs indicated,

(3) a message to the operator if available equipment will not be capable of maintaining adequate reserves while carrying forecast loads, and

(4) an alarm message if currently operating equipment fails to provide adequate reserves.

4. BUILDING-AUTOMATION SYSTEMS

For heating, air conditioning, lighting, and power, buildings consume more than 33% of all energy used in the United States. Most buildings now in use were designed and constructed when fuels and electrical power were readily available and inexpensive, and the need for energy conservation was not recognized. However, in recent years there has been a move to incorporate a section on minimum requirements for energy-efficient construction into the state building codes.

In general, most buildings are overheated in winter, overcooled in summer, overlighted and overventilated year round, and inefficiently operated. Each year they consume increasing amounts of energy because systems and building components deteriorate as maintenance and service become more costly and neglected.

Nationwide, the variable energy costs associated with HVAC and lighting systems can be ranked, in order of magnitude, as heating and ventilation, lighting, air conditioning and ventilation, equipment and processes, and domestic hot water.

However, the relative order of magnitude of energy use among the first three systems changes depending on climate, building construction, mode of operation and type of control, and equipment efficiency. The energy conservation approach in HVAC systems must focus first on the opportunity to specify, select, and configure energy-efficient equipment and systems and second, to install a building automation system that can enforce control and management procedures to minimize energy expenditure. The building automation system can range from a small programmable logic controller to an entire computer system for large campuses, hospitals, and institutions.

Computer systems have been used in building management systems either as off-line simulation modes or on-line real-time systems. Most off-line building management systems utilize buildings, as well as utility models, to simulate the operating conditions and obtain solutions to how the building complex can be operated to reduce energy costs. This type of system is often referred to as a building management advisory system.

The computer of an integral building management system has to perform tasks similar to that of an industrial plant. The energy conservation opportunities exist in utility generation, distribution, and consumption areas. In this case, the energy consumers are buildings, i.e., heating, cooling, lighting, and power for equipment.

The overall functions and capabilities for a real-time computer system may include utility-load management and control, e.g., economic dispatch of steam, electricity, and chilled water, energy accounting by metering these utilities (steam, chilled water, and electricity) for consumption, utility-generation optimization to reduce the purchased-energy costs, power-demand control and load-shedding programs to control kilowatt demand and reduce demand charges, and monitoring and control of building heating, ventilation, and air conditioning (HVAC) systems.

Some of the typical calculations necessary for energy management tasks are Btu calculations for steam, hot water, and chilled water, steam properties calculations (e.g., enthalpy, entropy and specific weight), and hourly degree-day computations based on input data from the weather station.

a. Utility Generation Optimization

The utility management and optimization techniques discussed in Chapters 5–7 can be applied to utility management and control for institutional buildings just as to industrial plants. Depending on complexity and operating constraints, the application technology can be tailored to individual situations to realize the minimum utility generation costs.

b. Peak-Demand Control and Load Shedding

Peak-demand control strategies including load-shedding programs are usually an important subset of the total energy management program. Section A in Chapter 6 describes in detail the current strategies and approaches. The computer system continuously monitors total electrical consumption, calculates demand, and limits peak demand by load shedding and/or cycling preselected loads on and off. The power-demand control program can provide the capability to progressively shed preselected loads in a priority sequence to share the peak demand, using a predicated peak-demand forecast program.

c. HVAC Management and Control

An HVAC management and control system is an integral part of the building automation system. It focuses on the system's capability to provide constant surveillance of all building systems to enable the most efficient and effective use of energy and manpower possible. A typical function performed by an HVAC management and control system is the monitoring of operating conditions of all systems to enforce an operating policy via local controllers to optimize energy use while satisfying the comfort of occupants and the requirements of air conditioning equipment.

To accomplish building automation and energy conservation tasks, the following functions are typically required of a computer system: fan start–stop, valve–damper–motor control, pump start–stop, zone temperature control, relative humidity control, economizer control, nighttime, weekend, and holiday scheduling, provision of load-shed resources for power-demand control, and enthalpy optimization.

d. System Reports

There are many useful reports associated with the HVAC management system. These reports can be made available to the users on a demand or periodic basis for display on CRTs as well as for hardcopy printers. Some of the typical reports are system-operating log (e.g., boilers, chillers, and turbogenerators), building operating-parameter log (e.g., temperatures, humidity, air flows and velocities), alarm summary of utility systems and buildings, alarm-limit summary, equipment-status summary (e.g., on or off, under computer control or manual, maintenance history), system-error summary, and historical-trend summary.

10

Plant Study Procedures for Energy Conservation Projects

Most plant capital projects require an analysis of all the benefits and economic impacts, e.g., the return on investment, before a request for expenditure is approved. The goal of this chapter is to give some ideas on how to proceed with developing an economic justification by conducting a plant study.

A plant study is usually conducted by an in-plant project team, outside energy consultants, equipment manufacturers, or some combination of these manpower resources and experts. It is important to establish the guidelines, assumptions, and anticipated results before the study is undertaken so that the upper management responsible for approving the necessary funding has a good understanding of the project from the beginning.

221

The forthcoming plant study material is developed and presented as a case history. A chemical plant is interested in investigating and developing the feasibility of a computer-based energy management system. The study's objective is the identification of areas of potential energy management application and documentation of the potential economic benefits. The study should include the utility complex as a major area of energy management application. The plant's management decides that the study should be conducted jointly by the plant personnel and an outside consulting company.

A survey was conducted at the chemical plant to determine the energy conservation potential in the utility area. The following areas were selected for engineering and economic analysis: steam generation, cooling towers, electrical power management, and waste incineration. The selection of these areas was made on the basis of the energy intensiveness of the processes and their inadequate instrumentation for automatic control and system optimization.

A. Steam Generation

There are three boilers rated for 250,000-lb/hr capacity, each firing natural gas as boiler fuel. The plant's load swings range from 450,000 to 600,000 lb/hr, and the three boilers are operated by equally allocating the individual boiler loads.

1. BOILER-LOAD ALLOCATION

The potential fuel savings to be gained by allocating the steam load among the three boilers is examined. The Nelder–Mead Simplex method for function minimization is used off-line with the boiler models. Efficiency versus load is obtained by regressing the boiler operating data. This technique is described in Chapter 3. The result of the boiler-load allocation study is shown in Table 10.1.

To establish trends, three computer runs were made for the plant steam demands of 450,000, 525,000, and 600,000 lb/hr. For these runs it is shown that at low loads the potential savings decrease and at higher loads the savings increase. This trend is dictated by the

TABLE 10.1
Boiler-Load Allocation: Computer Run Results for Boilers 1, 2, and 3

Boiler no.	Pre-opt. load	Opt. load	Initial cost	Optimum cost at 8500 hr/yr	Savings ($/hr)	Savings ($/yr)
Case no. 1						
1	150,000	161,333.0625				
2	150,000	124,450.6250				
3	150,000	107,560.0000				
Results			1669.7023	3.0373	1666.6650	26,120
Case no. 2						
1	175,002	182,521.5625				
2	175,002	151,359.5000				
3	175,002	191,124.9375				
Results			1955.8093	3.6855	1952.1237	31,327
Case no. 3						
1	199,998	200,037.0624				
2	199,998	180,037.0625				
3	199,998	219,919.8750				
Results			2245.6682	4.5451	2241.1230	37,839

boiler operating characteristics, i.e., efficiency is influenced by the boiler loads.

The steam demand of 600,000 lb/hr is selected as an average plant load and the net savings of $4.55/hr, or $37,839/yr, is reported as the annual potential fuel-cost savings. The net savings is the difference between the boiler operating costs pre-optimum load (pre-opt. load) and optimum load (opt. load). Figure 10.1 shows how an energy management computer would interface with the existing combustion-control system for boiler-load allocation.

2. REDUCING STACK OXYGEN

The following calculation was made to estimate the results of reducing stack O_2 content from 3 to 1.5%. This saving constitutes only the heat that could be recovered by not heating the combustion products from ambient temperature to a stack temperature of 450°F.

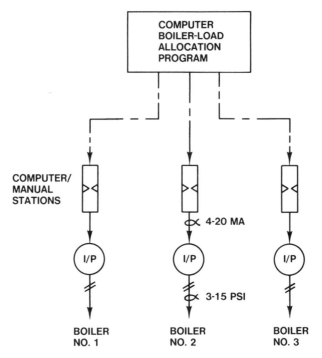

FIG. 10.1   Computer interface to existing pneumatic boiler master for load allocation.

Improved boiler efficiency that may occur by reducing stack temperature was not estimated.

First, the equation for the complete combustion of methane is written as

$$CH_4 + 2(1 + X)O_2 + 7.52(1 + X)N_2 \rightarrow CO_2 + 2H_2O + 2XO_2$$
$$+ 7.52(1 + X)N_2 + 344{,}032 \text{ Btu},$$

where X is the fraction of excess air and 7.52 moles of nitrogen accompany the oxygen. The liberated heat must be reduced by the heat of vaporization of the 2 moles of water to give an effective yield of 304,432 Btu's.

Because it is desirable to use a flue-gas analysis to determine the mole percentage of oxygen, a relation between excess air and oxygen must be made. This is done by directly computing the oxygen mole fraction, as

$$Y = \frac{\text{mole } O_2}{\text{total moles}} = \frac{2XO_2}{CO_2 + 2H_2O + 7.52(1 + X)N_2 + 2XO_2}$$

$$= \frac{2X}{10.52 + 9.52X},$$

where Y is the mole fraction of oxygen. Solving this equation for X gives

$$X = \frac{5.26Y}{5.26 - 4.76Y}.$$

Another equation is needed to compute the mass of the flue gas. By substituting the correct molecular weights into the combustion equation and dividing by the molecular weight of methane it can be shown that

$$M = 18.2 + 17.2X,$$

where M is the total mass of combustion products.

Table 10.2 shows the relationship between the mole fraction of oxygen in the flue gas, excess air, and amount of combustion products for 1 lb of methane.

TABLE 10.2

Relation between Mole Fraction Oxygen in the Flue Gas, Excess Air, and the Amount of Combustion Production[a]

O_2 in stack (%)	Product (lb)	Excess air (%)
0.0	18.20	0.00
0.5	18.66	2.69
1.0	19.15	5.52
1.5	19.66	8.50
2.0	20.20	11.63
2.5	20.77	14.93
3.0	21.37	18.41
3.5	22.00	22.09
4.0	22.67	25.99
4.5	23.38	30.12
5.0	24.14	34.51
5.5	24.94	39.19
6.0	25.80	44.18
12.0	43.52	147.20

[a] Heat yield (effective) is 19,252 Btu, with combustion of 1 lb of methane.

If the heat capacity of the flue gas is assumed to be about 0.225 Btu/lb°F, the energy savings can be calculated for any stack exit temperature as

$$Q = 0.225M(T_s - T_a),$$

where Q is the heat carried away by the combustion gases, M the gas flow rate, T_s the stack gas temperature, and T_a the ambient air temperature.

Table 10.3 shows the Btu losses for burning 1 lb of methane using a stack temperature of 450°F and an ambient temperature of 90°F. Using Table 10.3, it can be seen that by dropping the oxygen content from 3 to 1.5%, the percentage of loss drops by about 0.72%.

If the normal load is 525,000 lb/hr, then the annual operating cost can be estimated, using the following data: 8400 hr/yr, 85% boiler efficiency, $3.00/M Btu, and 893 Btu/lb heat of vaporization, as

$$525000 \, \frac{\text{lb}}{\text{hr}} \times 8400 \, \frac{\text{hr}}{\text{yr}} \times 893 \, \frac{\text{Btu}}{\text{lb}} \times \frac{\$3}{10^6 \, \text{Btu}} \times \frac{1}{0.85} = 13,899,282 \, \frac{\$}{\text{yr}}.$$

A 0.72% savings is $100,075.00/yr.

Figure 10.2 shows how an energy management computer would

TABLE 10.3
Btu Losses for Burning 1 lb of Methane[a]

O₂ in stack (%)	Btu removed by combustion gases	Heat loss (%)
0.0	1474	7.66
0.5	1511	7.85
1.0	1551	8.06
1.5	1592	8.27
2.0	1636	8.50
2.5	1682	8.74
3.0	1731	8.99
3.5	1782	9.26
4.0	1836	9.54
4.5	1894	9.84
5.0	1955	10.15
5.5	2020	10.49
6.0	2090	10.86

[a] Effective heat released is 19,252 Btu, with combustion of 1 lb of methane and stack temperature of 450°F and ambient temperature of 90°F.

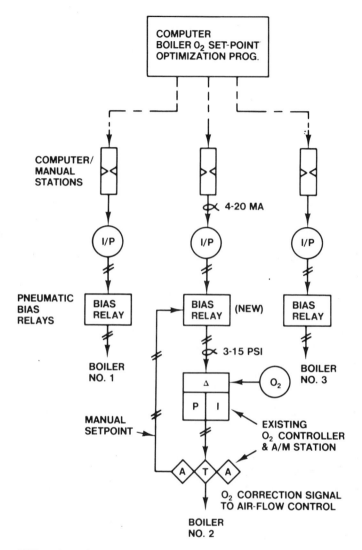

FIG. 10.2   Boiler O_2 set-point optimization program using a computer.

interface the existing oxygen controls to vary the oxygen set point for various loads determined by a load optimizer.

3. COMBUSTION-CONTROL ENHANCEMENT

Some enhancements can be made to the existing combustion-control systems to improve pressure control and response to rapid load changes.

The fuel and air cross-limit selectors, bias, and gain amplifiers have been recommended before the selectors. This, in effect, provides a "deadband" within which fuel and air are moved simultaneously for the fastest possible load-change response while still retaining the safety features of the cross-limited system on larger excursions. This function can be accomplished in the present system by adding pneumatic proportional relays for this purpose.

In addition, it would, of course, be desirable to eliminate pneumatic-transmission time lags in the metering signals, particularly the air flow. Pneumatic boosters could be added at the field-transmitter locations for this purpose or the existing transmitters could be replaced with equivalent electronic ones.

Another refinement for better pressure control would be the conversion of the plant master to a two-element type. This merely entails adding total plant steam flow as a feedforward signal to the master. This requires totalizing the three steam flows and adding a summing relay between the output of the plant master-pressure controller and the hand-auto station (plant master). This provides greater flexibility in tuning the controls to the requirements of the plant. The proportional action of the steam-flow feedforward signal on a load change provides initial positioning action to the fuel and air drives in approximately the correct amount for the new load point, and the pressure controller can then be fine tuned to provide the over- or under-firing necessary to achieve stability at the new load point with minimum pressure excursion.

The inability of the feedwater control to perform adequately under certain load-upset conditions was observed. The simplest solution to this is to move the feedwater-flow controller from the control room to the boiler area to eliminate pneumatic time lags. This normally corrects such situations.

B. Cooling-Tower Pump Operation

There are five identical cooling-water pumps driven by three electric and two steam turbine drives. To evaluate the effect of adding or deleting pumps to the system, a computer program was written to show the effect on the system pressure of varying the number and speed of the pumps for either fixed total flows or fixed system-friction factors. One of the constants required in operating the program is the utility cost for 1 hp on line for 8400 hr (1 yr) for either steam or electric drives. These constants are calculated as shown.

Electric hp:

$$1 \text{ hp} \times 8400 \frac{\text{hr}}{\text{yr}} \times 0.7457 \frac{\text{kW} \cdot \text{h}}{\text{hp} \cdot \text{hr}} \times \frac{\$0.032}{\text{kW} \cdot \text{h}} = \frac{\$200.44}{\text{yr}} \; ;$$

Steam hp (assuming exhaust steam is used by other units):

$$1 \text{ hp} \times 8400 \frac{\text{hr}}{\text{yr}} \times \frac{2545 \text{ Btu}}{\text{hp} \cdot \text{hr}} \times \frac{\$5.00}{10^6 \text{ Btu}} = \frac{\$106.89}{\text{yr}} \; .$$

(The \$5.00/MBtu is the result of assuming that the boiler is 85% efficient, that the turbine is 70% efficient, and that gas is \$3.00/ MBtu.)

Because the isentropic expansion of steam from 300 psia at 560°F to 120 psia will provide only 85 Btu's available for work out of approximately 1290 Btu's (about 6.6% work available), it is important that the exhaust steam be used for heat. Otherwise, the cost of 1 hp from a steam turbine is about \$1500/yr, which is 7.5 times the cost of electric drives.

Because throttling is possible for the steam turbines' pumps, calculations were made using fractional speeds on these pumps. The summary of the 26 cases is shown on Table 10.4. Table 10.5 shows an example of the detailed information for each case (e.g., Case No. 1). The following was used as a base case for calculating reduced pumping costs: for the minimum header pressure of about 75 psi, the analysis is based on $\frac{1}{3}$ yr, 40,000 gpm using five pumps at full speed (three electric, two turbines), $\frac{1}{3}$ yr, 35,000 gpm using four pumps at full speed (two electric, two turbines), and $\frac{1}{3}$ yr, 30,000 gpm using three pumps at full speed (one electric, two turbines). The costs in thousands of dollars per year are

TABLE 10.4
Summary of Pumping Costs

| Case no. | Flow (kg/min) | Pump speed | | Elec. motor #1 | Elec. motor #2 | Elec. motor #3 | Pres. (psig) | Annual operating cost ($1000) |
		Steam turbine 1	Steam turbine 2					
1	40	1.00	1.00	1.00	1.00	1.00	89.2	408
2	40	0.95	0.95	1.00	1.00	1.00	85.7	389
3	40	0.90	0.90	1.00	1.00	1.00	79.8	376
4	40	0.85	0.85	1.00	1.00	1.00	74.5	368
5	40	0.80	0.80	1.00	1.00	1.00	68.5	364
6	40	1.00	1.00	1.00	1.00	—	80.1	321
7	40	0.95	0.95	1.00	1.00	—	74.8	298
8	40	0.90	0.90	1.00	1.00	—	69.4	281
9	40	0.85	0.85	1.00	1.00	—	63.7	269
10	35	1.00	1.00	1.00	1.00	—	86.0	312
11	35	0.95	0.95	1.00	1.00	—	80.6	291
12	35	0.90	0.90	1.00	1.00	—	74.8	275
13	35	0.85	0.85	1.00	1.00	—	69.0	264
14	35	0.80	0.80	1.00	1.00	—	63.0	257
15	35	1.00	1.00	1.00	—	—	71.3	222
16	35	0.95	0.95	1.00	—	—	64.6	195
17	30	1.00	1.00	1.00	1.00	—	91.2	303
18	30	0.95	0.95	1.00	1.00	—	85.7	283
19	30	0.90	0.90	1.00	1.00	—	79.7	269
20	30	0.85	0.85	1.00	1.00	—	73.5	259
21	30	0.80	0.80	1.00	1.00	—	67.1	253
22	30	0.75	0.75	1.00	1.00	—	60.4	249
23	30	1.00	1.00	1.00	—	—	80.1	214
24	30	0.95	0.95	1.00	—	—	73.1	189
25	30	0.90	0.90	1.00	—	—	66.2	171
26	30	0.85	0.85	1.00	—	—	59.3	157

between case 1 and case 7:

$$\tfrac{1}{3} \times (408 - 298) = 36.7,$$

between case 10 and case 12:

$$\tfrac{1}{3} \times (312 - 275) = 12.3,$$

between case 23 and case 24:

$$\tfrac{1}{3} \times (214 - 189) = 8.3,$$

$$\text{total} = \$57,300/\text{yr.}$$

TABLE 10.5

A Detail of the Computer Runs on Pumping Cost Analysis (Case No. 1)[a]

Pump	Speed	Flow	Horsepower	Efficiency (%)	Cost ($1000/yr)
1 Steam	1	7996	510.55	81.4	51
2 Steam	1	7996	510.55	81.4	51
3 Electric	1	7996	510.55	81.4	102.1
4 Electric	1	7996	510.55	81.4	102.1
5 Electric	1	7996	510.55	81.4	102.1
Total		39,980	2522.75		

[a] Option 1, with specified flow at 40,000 gpm, back pressure at 89 psig. The annual cost is $408,000.

If a lower header pressure is possible, the savings can be increased. The pumping costs are related to the header pressure, but the actual costs depend on the interaction of the pumps with each other. Figure 10.3 shows a possible method of regulating header pressure.

C. In-Plant Generation

The plant has two turbogenerators of the multiple extracting/condensing type, rated at 10 MW each. It also has a contract with the local utility company to purchase electrical power through the tie-line. The contract limit is 7 MW.

Plant savings in the area of turbogeneration can be obtained through performance monitoring and extraction-flow optimization. Performance monitoring is determined by the completion of on-line calculations for each turbogenerator providing information to an operator for manual control and to the extraction-optimization portion of the energy management program in the computer for automatic control.

The performance of the turbogenerators can be determined by using the equations shown in Chapter 6 for heat rate, ideal heat rate, steam-path efficiency—combined and individual stage, mechanical efficiency, and overall efficiency.

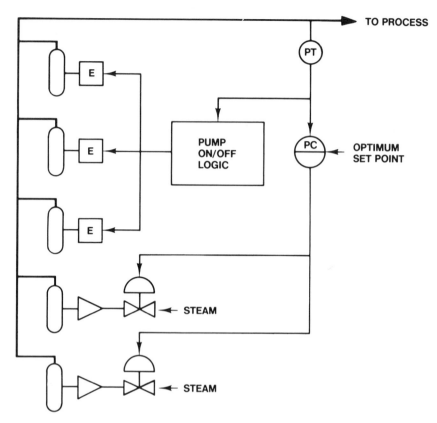

FIG. 10.3   One possible method of regulating header pressure.

Heat rate is the Btu's used per kilowatt-hour of electrical generation. By comparing the ideal rate with Btu's available per kilowatt-
hour for ideal conditions (isentropic expansion), a measure of performance is obtained. The combined steam-path efficiency is a ratio
of the actual heat rate to the ideal heat rate. Stage efficiency may be
calculated as the ratio of actual enthalpy change through the stage to
that for isentropic expansion. Losses caused by mechanical friction,
heat radiation, etc., are reflected in the mechanical efficiency, which
is the ratio of the Btu equivalent of 1 kW·h, 3412.7 Btu's, to the
actual Btu's used per kilowatt-hour generated. Overall, turbine efficiency is the product of combined steam-path efficiency and mechanical efficiency.

The fouling index is a relative value that allows the operator to easily compare the current heat-transfer rate to that achieved when the condenser was clean. Tie-line control can reduce energy costs by meeting plant steam demand by using the most optimum extraction leg of the turbogenerators (load allocation) and reducing the use of PRVs to achieve the maximum amount of electrical power per pound of steam and by meeting plant electrical demand by determining from the utility contract and cost data whether to purchase or generate by condensing. This will ensure that the peak demand is not exceeded while still providing the lowest-cost electricity.

Using the calculations discussed earlier to determine the heat rate, the cost of electrical generation is determined on-line by the computer using the calculation

$$GC = (HR \times SC \times KW + OE)/KW,$$

where GC is the generation cost in dollars per kilowatt-hour, HR the actual heat rate in Btu's per kilowatt-hour, SC the steam cost in dollars per Btu, OE the operating expense, which is fixed, and KW the generator output in kilowatts. This equation determines the cost per kilowatt-hour based on the heat rate, which is the number of Btu's used in producing 1 kW·h.

Data was chosen using a peak time, an intermediate-peak time, and an off-peak time for three different days (2:00 p.m., 7:00 p.m., and 4:00 a.m. were used for November 4, November 18, and December 2). These data were entered into the computer energy management program, and the resultant costs were calculated. Since the exhaust steam from the last stage of each turbogenerator was not known, saturation steam temperature was used. The exact river-water flow was not known so a figure of 11 million gal/day was used. The heat rate for both the turbogenerator and the heat lost through condensing were calculated and the total was used to determine the cost per kilowatt-hour for each time period.

Using these calculated costs, allocation and tie-line control savings were calculated. These calculations were based on meeting plant steam demand (using the same extraction flows) and reducing condensing to a minimum (i.e., 10,000 lb/hr). After determining the total kilowatts produced through extraction, the remaining plant kilowatt demand was met using 7000 kW for a purchase limit during intermediate and off-peak periods and 6000 during the peak periods.

TABLE 10.6
Base Case as Found Costs

Date	Time	T.G. #5 kW	¢/kW·h	$/hr	T.G. #6 kW	¢/kW·h	$/hr	Tie kW	¢/kW·h	$/hr	Total ($)
Nov. 4	2:00 p.m.	7200	5.41	389.77	5700	4.57	260.50	5600	3.29	184.24	834.51
	7:00 p.m.	7200	5.42	390.41	6200	4.86	301.65	4900	3.69	180.81	872.87
	4:00 a.m.	7600	5.39	409.68	6100	4.34	264.83	5400	2.99	161.46	835.97
Nov. 18	2:00 p.m.	7300	4.14	302.58	6800	5.08	315.34	4900	3.24	161.21	779.13
	7:00 p.m.	7000	4.71	329.80	5900	5.62	331.33	2500	3.69	92.25	753.38
	4:00 a.m.	7200	3.80	273.90	6500	5.30	344.16	4600	2.99	137.54	755.60
Dec. 2	2:00 p.m.	7700	4.76	366.62	6300	5.15	324.66	4900	3.29	161.21	852.49
	7:00 p.m.	7200	4.53	326.31	6300	5.02	316.40	5200	3.69	191.88	834.59
	4:00 a.m.	7200	4.35	313.20	6000	4.71	282.60	5000	2.99	149.50	745.30

TABLE 10.7
Optimum Turbogenerator Loading and Kilowatt Purchase via Tie-Line

Date	Time	Plant demand (kW)	Extraction amount #5 (kW)	Extraction amount #6 (kW)	Total extraction amount (kW)	Difference (kW)	Actual loading Tie	#5	#6
Nov. 4	2:00 p.m.	18,500	6000	5700	11,700	6800	6800	6000	5700
	7:00 p.m.	18,200	5800	5200	11,000	7200	6000	6000	6200
	4:00 a.m.	19,100	6000	6100	12,100	7000	7000	6000	6100
Nov. 18	2:00 p.m.	18,400	6400	5200	11,600	6800	6800	6400	5200
	7:00 p.m.	15,400	5400	4900	10,300	5100	5100	5400	4900
	4:00 a.m.	18,300	6500	5400	11,900	6400	6400	6500	5400
Dec. 2	2:00 p.m.	18,700	6500	5300	11,800	6900	6900	6500	5300
	7:00 p.m.	18,400	7000	5700	12,700	5700	5700	7000	5700
	4:00 a.m.	18,200	7000	5900	12,900	5300	5300	7000	5900

TABLE 10.8
Optimum Electrical Power Allocation and Costs

Date	Time	T.G. #5 kW	¢/kW·h	$/hr	T.G. #6 kW	¢/kW·h	$/hr	Tie kW	¢/kW·h	$/hr	Total ($)
Nov. 4	2:00 p.m.	6000	4.4306	265.84	5700	4.3668	248.91	6800	3.29	223.72	738.47
	7:00 p.m.	6000	4.3821	262.93	6200	3.9104	242.44	6000	3.69	221.40	726.77
	4:00 a.m.	6000	4.4746	268.48	6100	4.1429	252.72	7000	2.99	209.30	730.50
Nov. 18	2:00 p.m.	6400	4.4301	283.53	5200	4.6334	240.94	6800	3.24	223.72	748.19
	7:00 p.m.	5400	4.9231	265.85	4900	4.5048	220.74	5100	3.69	188.19	674.78
	4:00 a.m.	6500	4.4372	288.42	5400	4.5502	245.71	6400	2.99	191.36	725.49
Dec. 2	2:00 p.m.	6500	4.4423	288.75	5300	4.6041	244.02	6900	3.29	227.01	759.78
	7:00 p.m.	7000	4.2372	308.58	5700	4.3575	248.37	5700	3.69	210.33	767.28
	4:00 a.m.	7000	4.2195	295.36	5900	4.1502	244.86	5300	2.99	158.47	698.69

Tables 10.6–10.8 show the costs of meeting the plant demands: as-found costs, optimum loading, and optimized costs, respectively.

Table 10.9 summarizes the results of the electrical power management analysis and the potential savings that may be realized from a computer-based energy management system. The computer system with the electrical power management software automatically performs on-line allocation of the plant electrical loads.

D. Incinerator Controls

Energy can be saved at the incinerator by placing it in the stand-by mode if it is not burning wastes. The amount saved depends on the stand-by condition and the length of time at stand-by. The materials fed to the incinerator are

Material (waste)	Normal flow (gpm)	Max flow (gpm)
Tar	3	6
Organic	2–4	8
Aqueous	2–3	10

TABLE 10.9
A Summary of Potential Savings[a]

Date	Time	As-found cost ($)	Optimized costs ($)	Savings ($/hr)	Average ($/hr)
Nov. 4	2:00 p.m.	834.51	738.47	96.04	
	7:00 p.m.	872.87	726.77	109.20	103.57
	4:00 a.m.	835.97	730.50	105.47	
Nov. 18	2:00 p.m.	779.13	748.18	30.95	
	7:00 p.m.	753.38	674.77	78.61	46.55
	4:00 a.m.	755.60	725.49	30.11	
Dec. 2	2:00 p.m.	852.49	759.78	92.71	
	7:00 p.m.	834.59	767.29	67.30	68.87
	4:00 a.m.	745.30	698.70	46.60	

[a] Total average = $73.00 × 24 hr = $1751.93/day; annual (300 days) savings = $525,575.97.

It can be seen from the above table that the maximum normal flow is only 50% of the maximum possible flow. Therefore, it might be possible to feed at higher rates for shorter periods of time. Assume that 25% of the time it may be possible to idle the incenerator at 700°C exit temperature instead of the normal 1020°C and that 12% oxygen is present in the stack. Table 10.2 shows that for 12% stack oxygen, the mass flow of gas per pound of methane burned is 43.52 lb. The heat saving is

$$\frac{43.52 \text{ lb} \times 0.225 \text{ Btu/lb°F} \times 320°C \times 1.8°F/°C}{19,252 \text{ Btu}} = 0.293, \text{ or } 29.36\%.$$

The operating cost of the incinerator at 12,500 std. ft³/hr of gas is $315,000/yr. Reduction of 29% for 25% of the year is a 7.25% decrease, or a savings of $22,838/yr.

E. Summary

The areas selected and analyzed for potential energy conservation in the utilities were steam generation, cooling towers, electrical power management, and waste incineration. It was determined that there were five categories for savings. The estimated savings for these categories are listed in the tabulation.

Category	Estimated annual savings ($)
Boiler-load allocation	31,327
Reducing stack oxygen	100,075
Cooling-tower pump operation	57,300
Electrical power management	525,576
Waste incineration	22,838
Total savings	737,116

References

Andreasen, C., and Seemann, D. (1981). "Boiler Fuel Optimization Using an Intelligent Digital Plant Master and Boiler Master." Instrument Society of America 1981 Annual Conference and Exhibit, St. Louis, Missouri.

Bannister, R. L., Bellows, J. C., and Osborne, R. L. (1983). Steam turbine generators—on-line monitoring and availability. *Mechanical Engineering,* July, 55–59.

Blevins, T., Roberts, D., Block, L., and Andreasen, C. (1980). "A Standardized Software Package for Energy Monitoring and Energy System Optimization in the Pulp and Paper Industry." Instrument Society of America 1980 Annual Conference and Exhibit, Vol. 35, Part 1, 315–328.

Cho, C. H. (1978). Optimum boiler load allocation. *Instrumentation Technology,* October, 55–58.

Cho, C. H. (1981). Energy management applications for the steel industry. *Iron and Steel Engineer,* April, 54–60.

Cho, C. H. (1982a). "Efficient Allocation of Steam." Industrial Energy Conservation Manual 16, MIT Press, Cambridge, Massachusetts.

Cho, C. H. (1982b). "Measurement and Control of Liquid Level." An Independent Learning Module from the Instrument Society of America, Research Triangle Park, North Carolina.

Cho, C. H., and Blevins, T. (1980). Applying energy management in pulp and paper mills. *TAPPI Journal,* June, 91–94.

Cho, C. H., and Dray, B. (1982). Reducing demand and energy charges with an automatic demand controller. *Plant Engineering,* March 18, 213–216.

Cho, C. H., and Norden, B. N. (1982). Computer optimization of refrigeration systems in a textile plant—a case history. *Automatica* **18**(6), 675–683.

Clary, A. T. (1983). Using a microcomputer to perform steam balance calculations. *Mechanical Engineering,* July, 43–47.

Deliyannides, J. S. (1968). "Total Energy Allocation." Ph.D. Thesis, Electrical Engineering Department, The University of Pittsburgh, Pittsburgh, Pennsylvania.

Edgar, T. F. (1980). "Automatic Control Opportunities in Industrial Energy Utilization." Paper presented at the International Federation of Automatic Control Workshop, Houston, Texas.

Fisher Controls International (1977). "Pulp and Paper Technology Manual." Fisher Controls International, Marshalltown, Iowa.

Gorindan, T. S. (1982). "Energy Management: The Next Phase." Proceedings of the Refining Department of the American Petroleum Institute 47th Winter Meeting, Washington, D.C.

Gray, W. R., Fekete, J. D., and Tarkoff, M. I. (1974). A steel plant energy model. *Iron and Steel Engineer,* November, 54–59.

May, D. L. (1980). Cutting cost through automatic pump control. *Control Engineering,* November, 95–99.

May, D. L., Norden, B. N., Andreason, C. C., and Cho, C. H. (1979). Optimizing plant refrigeration costs. *Instrument Society of America Transactions* **18**(1), 71–79.

Michaelson, R. B., and Herrewig, M. T. (1983). "Wood/Oil Exchange Control for a Combined Fired Hog Fuel Boiler at MacMillan Bloedel Limited, Harmac Division." Proceedings of the Third International Pulp and Paper Process Control Symposium, Vancouver, B.C., Canada.

Nelder, J. A., and Mead, R. (1967). A Simplex Method for Function Minimization. *Computer Journal,* **7,** 308–313.

Shinskey, F. G. (1978). "Energy Conservation through Control." Academic Press, New York.

Stecco, S. S., Carnevale, E., Bona, M., and Paganelli, M. (1981). "Experiences and Trends in Textile Industry Energy Problems." Proceedings of the 4th World Energy Engineering Congress.

Uronen, P. (1980). "Toward Energy Self-Sufficiency in the Pulp and Paper Industry." Paper presented at the International Federation of Automatic Control Workshop, Houston, Texas.

U.S. Department of Energy (1979). "Computer Technology: Its Potential for Industrial Energy Conservation." DOE/CS/2/23-T2. National Technical Information Service, Springfield, Virginia.

Zimmer, H. (1975). "Chiller Control Using On-Line Allocation for Energy Conservation." Instrument Society of America 1975 Annual Conference, Houston, Texas.

Index